Defensive
Soccer Tactics

CONTENTS

Defensive Soccer Tactics

Jens Bangsbo

Birger Peitersen

Human Kinetics

Library of Congress Cataloging-in-Publication Data

Bangsbo, J. (Jens)
   [Vi forsvarer. English]
   Defensive soccer tactics / Jens Bangsbo, Birger Peitersen
     p. cm.
   "Revised edition of Vi forsvarer, published in 1998 by Forlaget Hovedland"--T.p. verso.
   ISBN 0-7360-3272-X
    1. Soccer--Defense.   2. Soccer--Coaching.   I. Peitersen, Birger.   II. Title.
   GV943.9.D43 B33   2002
   796.334'2--dc21   2001051557

ISBN: 0-7360-3272-X

This book is a revised edition of *Vi Forsvarer,* published in 1998 by Forlaget Hovedland.

Acquisitions Editor: Todd Jensen; **Developmental Editor**: Leigh LaHood; **Copyeditor**: Marc Jennings; **Proofreader**: Kathy Bennett; **Graphic Designer**: Nancy Rasmus; **Graphic Artist**: Sandra Meier; **Cover Designer**: Keith Blomberg; **Photographer (cover)**: Empics Sports Photo Agency; **Photographer (interior)**: © Per Kjaerbye Pressefotograf; **Illustrators**: Tom Roberts and Tara Welsch; **Printer**: Bang Printing

Human Kinetics books are available at special discounts for bulk purchase. Special editions or book excerpts can also be created to specification. For details, contact the Special Sales Manager at Human Kinetics.

Printed in the United States of America   10 9 8 7 6 5 4 3 2 1

Human Kinetics
Web site: www.humankinetics.com

United States: Human Kinetics
P.O. Box 5076, Champaign, IL 61825-5076
800-747-4457
e-mail: humank@hkusa.com

Canada: Human Kinetics
475 Devonshire Road Unit 100, Windsor, ON N8Y 2L5
800-465-7301 (in Canada only)
e-mail: orders@hkcanada.com

Europe: Human Kinetics
Units C2/C3 Wira Business Park, West Park Ring Road, Leeds LS16 6EB, United Kingdom
+44 (0) 113 278 1708
e-mail: hk@hkeurope.com

Australia: Human Kinetics
57A Price Avenue, Lower Mitcham, South Australia 5062
08 8277 1555
e-mail: liahka@senet.com.au

New Zealand: Human Kinetics
P.O. Box 105-231, Auckland Central
09-523-3462
e-mail: hkp@ihug.co.nz

Key to Diagrams

● ● ○   Players

⚽   Ball

∿∿➤   Path of player dribbling the ball

- - - - ➤   Path of player without the ball

———➤   Path of the ball

INTRODUCTION

Modern soccer is vilified for being defense-heavy. As described in the book *Soccer Systems & Strategies*, it is a fact that, through the years, more and more players have gradually been pushed from attack to defense. In this respect, it is correct that starting formations are more defense-oriented now than previously. On the other hand, the tasks and roles of individual players are more comprehensive today than in earlier times. While the tasks of a defender in the 1950s and 1960s were extremely limited, there are now various all-around defensive and attacking tasks that apply to all players. For this reason, the numeric distribution of players in a formation (e.g., 4-4-2) no longer denotes a clear defensive or offensive direction of play.

The old military proverb "A good defense is the best basis for a good attack" is the motto of many elite-level coaches. There is an ongoing debate about the relationship between the coach's soccer philosophy and the style of play practiced by that coach's team. A common question in this discussion is whether a team is offensive or defensive. In the book *The Ambassador*, former Real Madrid coach Jorge Valdano says that he sees the doom of soccer in his "ultra-realist" colleagues. These people cannot dream, and only strengthen his faith in his own concept of soccer, which he expresses thus: "Some people say that soccer is only about winning. Other, happier people, maintain that it is also about joy." Soccer is under attack from the results faction, and it is these people who ask why we need to play well. It is refreshing to refer to the poet Borges, who was asked what the use of poetry was. "What is a caress good for? What is the aroma of coffee good for? Each question is like an answer. It is for pleasure, it is for emotion, it is for life!"

At times, a well-coordinated defense generates pleasure. When defensive work comes off, we talk about it "looking good." As inherent factors in this, the defense must be prepared for the opposition's challenges, and the individual player must feel that his defensive contribution means something to the other players. For a defender, there are various rewards, such as the euphoria when a tackle goes perfectly, or when he springs into the air with impeccable timing to win a head-to-head with an opponent. This satisfaction affects the whole team, as does the feeling of success when the opposition tries in vain to break through, each time prevented by astute defensive action. A well-organized defense will generally provide a team with the best preparation for attacking play.

In this book, we provide the necessary impulse and inspiration to help the coach develop a better, well-organized defense. If you, as coach, can persuade the players to see defense as responsible and rewarding, and not as a boring necessity, you will have a well-balanced team whose potential will increase substantially.

To a great extent, the defensive game depends on both the actions of the individual and coordination between the players. Defenders must quickly understand each other's reactions, particularly when they are under pressure, as illustrated here by Sol Campbell's screening of the ball until the goalkeeper, David Seaman, can secure it.

CHAPTER I

Covering and Marking

The basic elements in individual defensive work are covering—a general description of a player's actions when the opposing team has the ball—and marking, which denotes defensive work against a direct opponent. This chapter will explain these concepts and provide training suggestions.

When the opposition has the ball, the defending team's players must create conditions for regaining it. The contributions a player makes toward this are in covering and marking, which are inherent factors in defensive work everywhere on the pitch, regardless of whether a team is playing with zonal or man-to-man cover.

A team often has one or more players whose primary task is to cover the front opponents, which is why they are often called markers. Typical markers among Danish internationals of recent times have included Søren Busk, Ivan Nielsen, and Marc Rieper, whose main task was to tightly mark a striker on the opposing team.

Goals

- To prevent opponents from receiving the ball in a favorable position.
- To prevent the player with the ball from shooting, passing, or dribbling the ball upfield.
- To be able to win the ball.
- To force play in a certain direction.

The player receiving the ball should be unable to turn in the attacking direction. Here, Nigeria's Usche Ucheshukwo is marking the Danish player Peter Møller tightly to prevent him from doing just that.

Fundamentals

When the opposition wins the ball, it is up to the defending team's players to take up appropriate defensive positions and create the best conditions for regaining the ball. To achieve this, players must act in accordance with several fundamentals of the game, as described in the following section.

Retreat

At the moment when a team loses possession, several players will be ahead of the ball. The players around the ball should, therefore, quickly move defense-side; that is, they should be closer to their own goal than the ball is. Players who are a long way up the pitch should move closer to their own goal than their nearest opponents are (see figure 1.1). When a team is facing a counterattack, the wingers should run back in the direction of their near post, while the midfield players should head toward the penalty spot (see figure 1.2). When moving toward a direct opponent, a player should sprint to within about two meters of the opponent and then slow down to ensure the ability to react if the opponent tries to get past.

Positioning

When marking an opponent, a player should take up a position on a line between his own goal and the attacking player. In doing this, he should turn slightly away from his opponent so he can see both the ball and the opponent, "splitting" his vision. From this position, a player can win the ball before it reaches the opponent. How close a defender should be to the attacking player depends on the angle between the ball, the opponent, and the goal. If the player with the ball can "see" the goal, and the defender and the opponent are between the goal and that player, the defender should stand almost as far back as the attacker. This is to prevent the direct opponent, on receiving the ball, from taking it past the defender. However, if the player with the ball is out on the wing, the defender can stand beside the direct opponent, facing the player with the ball and keeping both opponents in view (see figure 1.3 on page 6). A defender out on the wing can also take position beside the opponent. For example, the black number 2 in figure 1.4 on page 7 can take up a position to the left of white 10 because this offers a better chance of reaching the ball first in the event of a pass to 10. If the pass is put into the free area along the sideline, 2 will be able to limit 10's options.

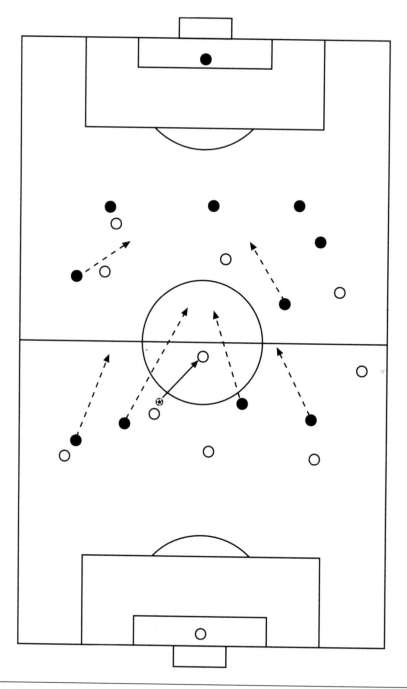

Figure 1.1 Players retreating closer to their own goal than their nearest opponents are to the goal.

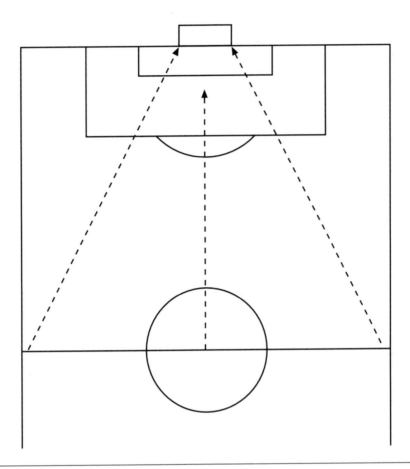

Figure 1.2 Paths of retreat for wingers and midfield players.

Defensive Position

When defending, the player should aim for a low center of gravity by bending the knees and hips slightly (limbs in the intermediate position). One leg should be in front of the other, pulling the body in line with the ball. This position makes it easier for the defender to change direction, but it also means taking small steps. Consider international Danish player Jan Heintze: He is a player who combines positioning ability and the appropriate defensive position.

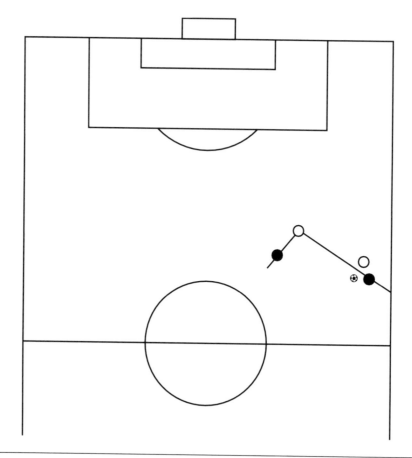

Figure 1.3 The defender keeps in sight his nearest opponent and the player with the ball, who is on the wing.

Distance

When a player is marking, the distance between that player and a direct opponent will depend on where the ball is. If the ball is close to the players, the marker should be within about one half to one meter of the opponent. If the opponent is fast, however, it may be necessary to stand at a distance of one to two meters, preventing the player from breaking free of the marker if the ball is played right forward. When the ball comes to a marker's direct opponent, it is vital for the marker to close down the opponent quickly, preventing the offensive player from turning in the attacking direction. When the ball is on the opposite side of the pitch, the marking player should not be too close to a direct opponent. In that

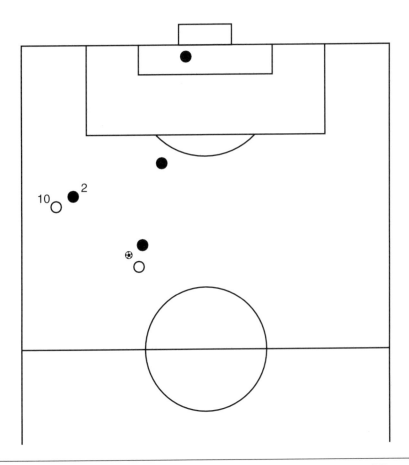

Figure 1.4   The defender on the wing (2) positioning himself beside his opponent (10).

situation, the marker should move into the center of the pitch, maintaining a distance that allows both backing up a teammate and reaching a direct opponent who gets the ball on a pass (see figure 1.5).

Winning the Ball

Defenders can win the ball from an opponent through tackling, by nudging the ball away from the player, or by intercepting a pass. International soccer demonstrates that defenders win balls more and more by blocking passes and to a lesser extent by tackling the player with the ball. Blocking passes is the most effective way of winning the ball. On one hand, the ball winner moves in front of the opponent as if intending to pass by, and on the

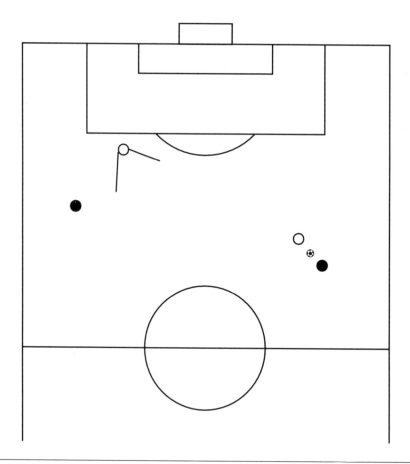

Figure 1.5 From this position, the marking player can either back up his teammate or reach his opponent if the ball is passed to him.

other hand this player is moving forward, enabling teammates to counter more swiftly. The defender should always be aware of the opposition's next passing option. A player's speed is determined to a great extent by the ability to understand ways in which a game situation may develop.

A defender attempting a tackle can lay the foundation for success. By assessing how the opponent can be expected to receive and bring down the ball, the defender can get in position for a tackle as soon as the opponent touches the ball. If the player receiving the ball controls it, the defender can feint a tackle, enticing the opponent to move the ball so that it can be nudged away or the opponent tackled. As with all attempts to win the ball, the defender must stay standing. A player who goes into a tackle

The defender must maintain an appropriate distance between himself and the player with the ball, to avoid being easily outplayed. Here, the Brazilian midfielder, Dunga, is too close to Denmark's Michael Laudrup, who passes him.

by diving at the ball will often leave an empty space for the opponent if the attempt fails. A defender on the ground can cover neither an opponent nor an area. A sliding tackle will always be a gamble and, if unsuccessful, may cost the defender dearly. Jes Høgh, for example, conceded a penalty against France in the 1998 World Cup when he took a chance and ran into a French attacker who nudged the ball past his sliding feet. The sliding tackle can, however, be used around the edges of the pitch if an opponent is on the point of escaping.

A sliding tackle is a gamble, but in this case Nemec succeeds in nudging the ball away from Thomas Hässler.

Determining Direction

A defender can use position to force the player with the ball in a certain direction. If the defender faces the player with the ball, the latter can move sideways and backward. The defender who gets positioned a little to one side and turns slightly will more or less "force" the opponent in the direction the defender's stance suggests. Chapter 3 more fully explains this defensive action.

Practices and Drills

When coaching marking, it is important to establish a definite attacking direction, to enable defenders to take up appropriate positions. In addition, it is often advantageous to have lots of small "goals" so that the markers gain nothing from retreating to protect one goal.

Teams whose defenders are not quick enough to cover an opponent's shooting side in the area are often punished. This cost the Czech Republic the gold in the final against Germany in 1996, when Oliver Bierhoff scored a golden goal.

Many of the exercises relating to support and recovery (in chapter 2) contain marking tasks and can be used for marking practice without making any vital changes. For example, the drill, Short Passes (on page 50), is suited to marking practice. We have provided more exercises in the following section. The first three drills are useful as warm-up exercises.

Warm-Up Dribbling

Players

Two.

Description

Meandering slightly, 1 dribbles slowly forward from the centerline to the goal line. Player 2 tracks backward, trying to maintain the distance from 1. When they reach the goal line, they switch. They can vary the tempo. See figure 1.6.

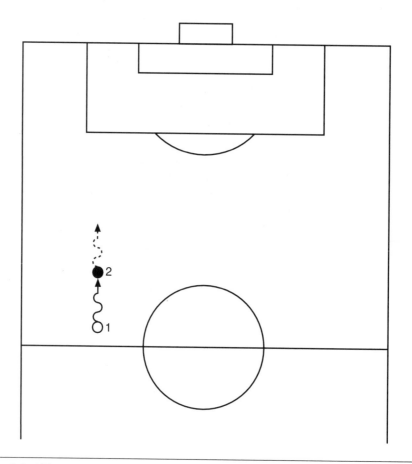

Figure 1.6   Warm-up dribbling.

Steal the Ball

Pitch

Penalty area.

Players

Eight: four versus four.

Description

The players on the white team each have a ball. Each white-team player is marked by a black-team player who is trying to win the ball (see figure 1.7). If successful, the black-team player dribbles out to the sidelines as quickly as possible and leaves the ball there, then heads back onto the field. Meanwhile, a white-team player with a ball pairs up with the player who lost the ball. The black player coming back on the field joins a teammate, and they play against the white pair. The other players continue one on one until another black player wins a ball. If the white pair loses their ball, both black players should play the ball out to the sidelines.

The next time the black team wins a ball, a three-versus-two situation arises during the transition phase. When the black-team players win the last ball, they begin again with four balls. The team that maintains possession the longest is the winner.

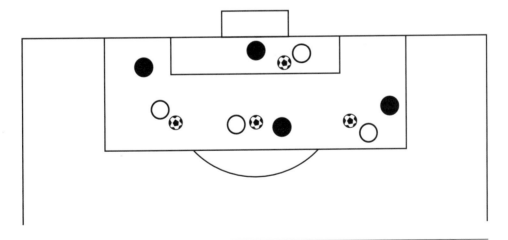

Figure 1.7   Steal the ball.

One-on-One in a Circle

Players

Six: five attackers (1-5) and one marker (6).

Organization

Four attackers (1-4) stand with a ball each outside a circular area; 5 and 6 are inside this area.

Description

The exercise is divided into three phases:

Phase one: Players 1-4 take turns passing to 5, who plays back with the first touch. Player 6 should shadow 5 relatively passively. See figure 1.8.

Phase two: There are no set passing patterns. Player 5 should break free from the marker to receive and return a pass. The marker is fully active and should prevent these double passes. A double pass is worth one point. How many points can 5 score within a set time limit—say, 30 seconds?

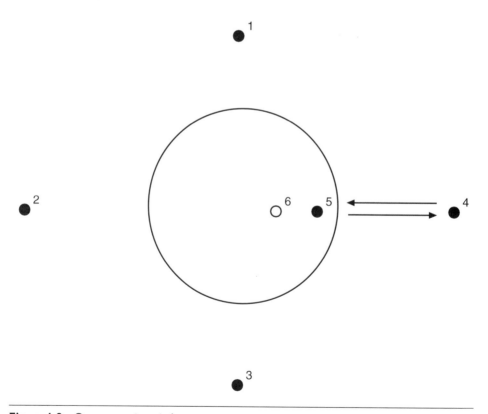

Figure 1.8 One-on-one in a circle.

Phase three: Only half of the players outside the area have a ball. The players in the area (5 and 6) now take turns at being the attacker and the marker—meaning they play against each other. The attacker no longer needs to play the ball first time. The attacker scores one point on receiving the ball from a player outside the area, and another on playing the ball back out of the area to a player without a ball. The pass must be precise for this point to be ratified (the outer players could have their own zones). The same player maintains possession until losing the ball, which is defined as being when the ball is won or when a pass to an outer player is intercepted. The players outside the area should always be ready to pass the ball to the player inside the area.

Variations

1. Several attackers and markers are in the area. In phase three, form two teams that play together inside the area.

2. In phase three, it's illegal to play the ball back to the player passing it into the area.

Three-Zone Marking

Pitch

Approximately one fifth of the pitch (an extended penalty area) consisting of three zones (1-3) and one large goal.

Players

Four: one midfielder (7), one striker (10), one defender (3), and a goalkeeper (1).

Description

Player 7 passes to 10, who should try to dribble past 3 and shoot. See figure 1.9 for the player positions.

Conditions

Players 3 and 10 are only allowed in zones 1 and 2; player 7 must stay in zone 3.

Scoring

As normal.

Variations

1. Player 10 may use 7 in a one-two.
2. Player 10 should play to 7, who is allowed no more than two touches.
3. Players 3 and 10 are only allowed in zone 1 (the penalty area). The goalkeeper may not leave his area.

Coaching Points

This exercise focuses on the distance between 3 and 10, and 3's position relative to 10. Player 3 should become aware of the problems arising from standing close by the opponent (the attacker can break away from the marker) or at a distance from the opponent (the attacker can turn).

During variations one and two, player 3 should become accustomed to moving and changing position quickly, and taking up the correct position relative to 10 and the passing angle from 7. Furthermore, 3 should become aware of the dangers involved in losing the opponent instead of covering the pass.

Variation three focuses on player 3's marking tactics when the ball is a little farther away. To what degree should 3 gamble on winning the pass from 7, with the risk that 10 may turn or receive the ball on the other side of 3?

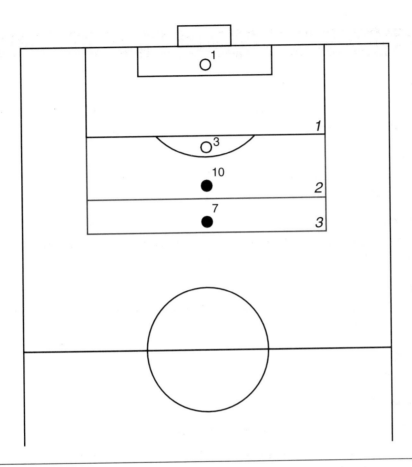

Figure 1.9   Three-zone marking.

Keywords

Retreat • Positioning • Defensive position • Distance • Ball winning • Determine the direction

Defensive Intervention

Pitch

One eighth of the pitch.

Players

Four.

Organization

Two players (1 and 4) are on the sidelines, and 1 has the ball. One player is behind each baseline (2 and 3). Rotate after each game with 1 taking 2's position and 2 taking 3's position. Player 3 moves out behind 4.

Description

Player 1 passes to 2, who runs to meet the ball and tries to dribble it over the opposite goal line. Player 3 should prevent 2 from dribbling the ball over the goal line. See figure 1.10.

Scoring

Players score by dribbling the ball over the boundary line.

Variations

1. The pass to 2 is played in the air.
2. Player 3 starts from inside the pitch.

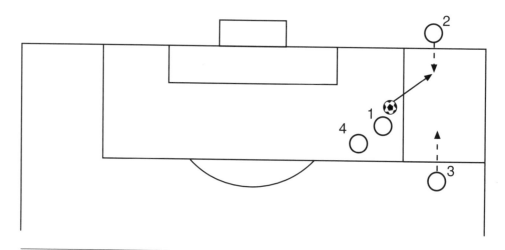

Figure 1.10 Defensive intervention.

Coaching Points

This exercise focuses on defensive action. The defender should time movements relative to the player with the ball, take up a position to put the intended pressure on that player, and judge when to tackle. Player 3 must accelerate toward 2 and, about two to three meters away, be in the appropriate defensive position, turned to entice 2 to dribble in the desired direction. If 3's approach is too fast, 2 will find it easy to dribble past 3.

In variation one, it may be more difficult for the player receiving the ball to control it. This will give 3 more time to find an appropriate defensive position.

In variation two, 3 is so close to 2 that it will be necessary to judge the timing of the intervention according to how difficult the pass is. When 3 breaks forward quickly, there is a chance of capturing the ball quickly, but also an increased risk of being outplayed, say, by the opponent running wide.

Keywords

Retreat • Positioning • Defensive position • Distance • Ball winning • Determine the direction

Find Your Position

Pitch

One quarter of the pitch, divided into two zones (1 and 2) with one large goal.

Players

Nine: four versus four, and a goalkeeper.

Organization

Two players (white 3 and black 10) in zone 1, with the other players in zone 2, except 8 who is behind the centerline.

Description

Two players from the white team start with the ball in zone 2; they must try to keep it within this zone. Three black players try to win the ball. (See figure 1.11.) When they win the ball, they should play it forward within two passes to black 10, after which play is unrestricted. White 8 will defend if teammates in zone 2 lose the ball.

Scoring

The black team scores in the large goal, while the white-team players, once they have regained the ball, can score by playing white 8 when this player is on the other side of the centerline again.

Variations

1. Another player for each team join the others in zone 2.
2. Move the zones forward into the opposition's half of the field (see figure 1.12).

Coaching Points

This exercise teaches the players on the white team to find appropriate defensive positions. When they lose the ball, the white players should retreat from zone 2 into a position closer to their own goal than the ball. White 8 should move closer to the white goal than the nearest opponent is. It is vital that the first white player to go after the player with the ball try to harry the attacker as much as possible, thereby winning time for the defender's teammates to get back. For example, this player could apply so much pressure that the attacker has difficulty keeping the ball under control or may be forced out onto the wing.

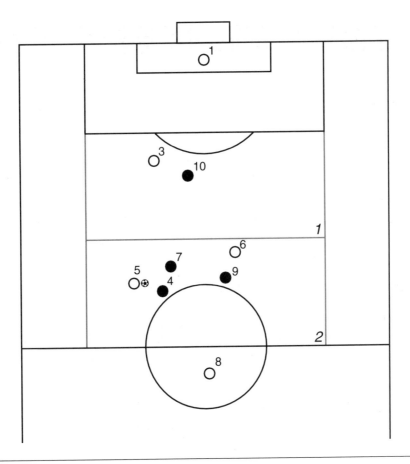

Figure 1.11 Find your position.

Variation one increases the black team's chances of quickly moving the game into the finishing area, putting more pressure on the white team's retreat.

In variation two, the focus is on retreating runs farther up the pitch. This means that white 8's starting position is in the opposition's penalty area, while the black team's scoring options are different. The black team now scores by dribbling the ball over one of the two three-meter-wide cone goals on the centerline (see figure 1.12).

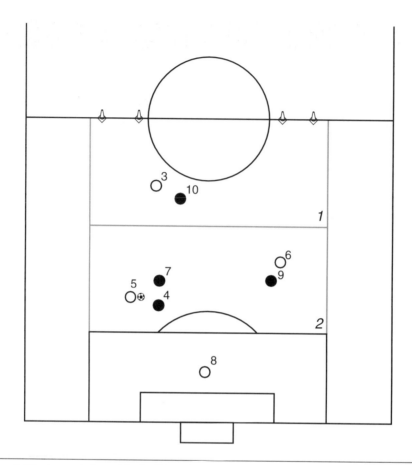

Figure 1.12 In a variation of the Find Your Position drill, the zones can be moved forward into the opposition's half of the field.

Keywords

Retreat • Positioning • Defensive position • Distance • Ball winning • Determine the direction

Hit the Cones

Pitch

About 20×16.5 meters, consisting of two zones (1 and 2); goals (cones) are on the baselines of zones 1 and 2.

Players

Six: three versus three.

Organization

Each team has one player in zone 1 and two players in zone 2. See figure 1.13.

Description

Normal game; each defensive player is responsible for a zone and an opponent. Defenders should tightly mark their opponents.

Conditions

The players must remain in their starting zones.

Scoring

Players score points by hitting the opposition's cones.

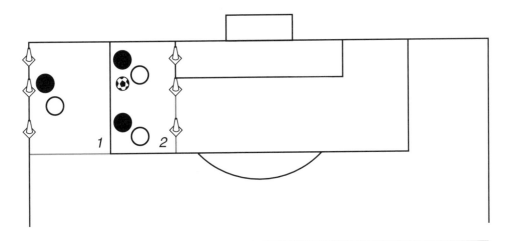

Figure 1.13 Hit the cones.

Variations

1. Once during each attacking phase, one player from the attacking zone may switch with someone in the defensive zone. The defenders can decide for themselves which players they want to mark.

2. The defenders may have no more than two touches and no more than two passes among themselves within the defensive zone.

Coaching Points

This game focuses on the basic moves involved in marking, namely the positions of the defenders and their distance from their opponents. Encourage the attacking players to move around a lot (even when the opposing team has the ball) so that the task of marking becomes more difficult.

In variation one, emphasize the changeover when defenders swap opponents.

You can use variation two if the game is too slow and is producing too few of the requisite marking situations.

Keywords

Retreat • Positioning • Defensive position • Distance • Ball winning • Determine the direction

One-on-One Cone Drill

Pitch

Optional size.

Players

Two: one versus one.

Organization

Four cones are positioned as shown in figure 1.14. The two near cones should be about six meters apart and the far ones about 20 meters apart. Each player defends two cones.

Description

The players should try to knock over their opponent's near or far cone. When someone scores, the players switch cones.

Scoring

Players score by knocking over the opponent's cone.

Variations

1. You can vary the distance between the cones.
2. You can play two versus two.

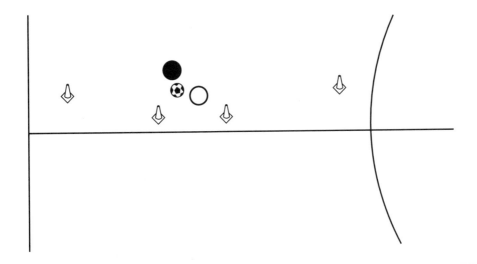

Figure 1.14   One-on-one cone drill.

Coaching Points

This game trains one-on-one situations and concentrates on ball-winning techniques and tactics. Players have to practice the basic principles of marking, constantly adjusting position in relation to the player with the ball due to the two scoring options.

When someone scores, the two players should walk slowly across to their new pair of cones, to prevent the exercise from exhausting them physically.

Variation one enables you to adapt the playing environment. If you move the cones farther apart, the exercise becomes more physically demanding.

In variation two, the two defenders must constantly readjust their tasks concerning who should pressure the player with the ball and who should support. The emphasis is also on winning the ball during a pass.

Keywords

Retreat • Positioning • Defensive position • Distance • Ball winning • Determine the direction

Three Zones, Six Goals

Pitch

Approximately one quarter of the pitch, divided into three zones (1-3). Position three small goals on the baselines of zones 1 and 3.

Players

Fourteen: seven versus seven.

Organization

Position three players from each team in zones 1 and 3, with one player from each team in zone 2 (center zone player). See figure 1.15 for positioning.

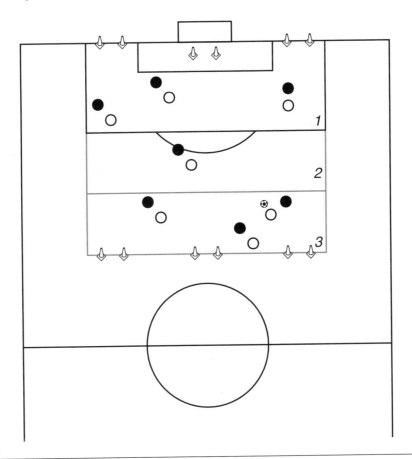

Figure 1.15   Three zones, six goals drill.

Description

Normal game; the ball must be played through the center zone (2) before being passed into the attacking zone (1 or 3).

Conditions

Players must remain in their starting zones.

Scoring

Goals are scored in one of the opposition's three small goals.

Variations

1. Two players from each team are in the center zone (2).
2. All players except the center zone players may go anywhere on the pitch; however, only the center zone players may touch the ball in the center zone.

Coaching Points

If the opposition wins the ball, all the players in the defensive zone can mark a player on the opposing team. This enables you to focus on how the markers can prevent their opponents from receiving the ball or from turning and playing a ball on. In addition, you can highlight the way the markers have to switch from attack to defense. The situation can change rapidly, so it is important to remain close to the opponent. The size of the center zone can determine the demands made on the markers there—the larger the center zone, the more difficult it will become for the markers.

The variations complicate the exercise, thus making the task of the markers more difficult. In variation one, all attackers need to mark tightly; in variation two, this applies to all players.

Keywords

Retreat • Positioning • Defensive position • Distance • Ball winning • Determine the direction

Four-Zone Game

Pitch

One half of the pitch, with two penalty areas (1 and 4), a center zone divided into two halves (2 and 3), and two large goals.

Players

Ten: four versus four and two goalkeepers.

Organization

Both teams position one player in each of the four zones. See figure 1.16.

Description

Normal game.

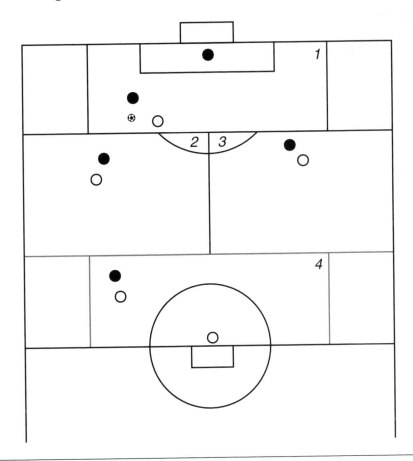

Figure 1.16   Four-zone game.

Conditions

Players may not leave their zones.

Scoring

As normal in the large goals.

Variations

1. When a team scores, the game—and attacking direction—reverses.
2. Two players from each team may be in one zone at the same time. However, the players in zones 1 and 4 (penalty areas) may not go into the opposing team's zones 4 or 1, respectively (i.e., the opponent's penalty area).
3. Two extra players join each side. These players may move freely around the pitch.

Coaching Points

As the playing area for each player is limited, this game provides a great opportunity for focusing on how players mark a direct opponent.

In variation one you can highlight the transition from attack to defense.

Variation two increases the players' need for good observation skills. In the attacking phase, the players at the back should participate in the upfield play while keeping one eye on the players they need to mark. In the defensive phase, the players should judge when to evade their markers and support a teammate.

Variation three places further demands on the observation skills of the players.

Keywords

Retreat • Positioning • Defensive position • Distance • Ball winning • Determine the direction

Pressure Marking

Pitch

Approximately one fifth of the pitch, divided into three zones—two outer zones (1 and 3), and one center zone (2).

Players

Ten: five versus five.

Organization

Both teams have one player in each of the outer zones (1 and 3). The remaining three players on each team are in the center zone (2). See figure 1.17.

Description

Each player in the center zone has a marking task.

Conditions

Players may not leave their zones.

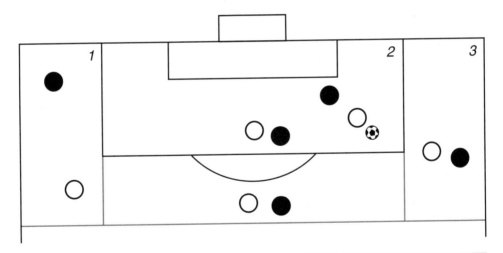

Figure 1.17 Pressure marking.

Scoring

Teams score a point by playing the ball from one outer zone to the other and then back to the first without the opposing team winning the ball. "Winning the ball" is defined as being when two players on the opposing team have touched the ball in succession.

Variations

1. The players in the center zone may also go into the outer zones.
2. The players in the center zone do not have set marking tasks.

Coaching Points

This exercise enables you to concentrate on the positions of the markers in relation to their opponents and the player with the ball, and on when the markers—particularly the players in the outer zones—should try to intercept passes to their direct opponents. You can also stress the importance of timing in leaving a marking task to help a teammate.

In variation one, the game area is extended, stretching the orientation skills of the players.

Variation two will accustom players to heading for markers after their team has a shot or loses the ball. During this phase, you can also focus on how communication between defenders can help in defensive work and can reduce the physical burden on individual players.

Keywords

Retreat • Positioning • Defensive position • Distance • Ball winning • Determine the direction

CHAPTER 2

Support and Recovery

A team with an efficient defense always seems to have lots of players around the ball. As a rule, this is due to the systematic development of the team's defensive game. A vital factor in whether a team's defensive work hangs together is that the players perform their individual defensive tasks, and they perform them with an understanding of their teammates' defensive tasks. This requires systematic training in defensive principles, providing simple ways in which the players can work together when defending. It is important to differentiate between the various defensive principles. Support, for example, is a prerequisite for most of the others. This means that when practicing one defensive principle, we must also use—and understand—other defensive principles.

In this chapter and chapter 3, we will explain the various defensive principles and recommend exercises for coaching them. Chapters 4 through 10 on the defensive game describe complex practices, working with several defensive principles at once. These sessions can help in the transition from isolated practice of one defensive principle to its application in a match situation. You can also use these exercises as refreshers if you've previously practiced one or more of the defensive principles. After you've introduced a defensive principle, you should give the players the opportunity to try it out in a game on a full-size pitch. During the game, you can point out when the relevant defensive principle can be used. Chapter 4—"Tactical Training"—in the book *Soccer Systems & Strategies* describes several ways you can vary instructions and methods of instruction.

Purpose of Support and Recovery

With the principle of support, a player takes a position behind one or more teammates to be able to intervene if the opponent plays or dribbles the ball past them (figure 2.1). With recovery, a player heads back to a position of support for one or more teammates (figure 2.2).

The principles of support and recovery are the concern of every player and can be applicable anywhere on the pitch; however, they are primarily used in the defensive half. Players always have support tasks during a match. For the sweeper, support is the primary defensive role. The sweeper should "read the game" and be ready to intervene if a teammate is outplayed.

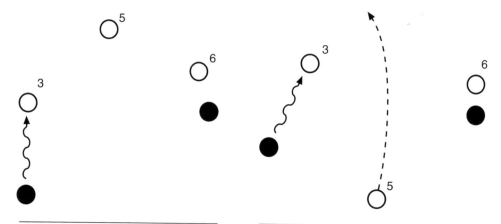

Figure 2.1 Player 5 supports teammates 3 and 6 by being in position behind them, available to intervene if the ball is played past them.

Figure 2.2 Player 5 demonstrates recovery by moving back to a position of support.

Goals

- To deny an opponent a free run with the ball after a teammate has been passed or outplayed.
- To regain the ball when an opponent has likewise passed a teammate or has played the ball some distance ahead.
- To win the ball when it is played into a free area.
- To allow teammates another opportunity to pressure the player in possession.
- To limit the development options for a skillful dribbler.

Support Fundamentals

The following main points are important for players to consider during a game—and for you when coaching the support principle.

Positioning

The support player should take up a position almost in a straight line between the player in possession or, if on the attack, a teammate, and the goal.

Distance

The distance between the support player and teammate(s) depends on the player's own speed and that of the attacker, as well as the attacker's dribbling abilities (technical expertise), the number of opponents and teammates in the surrounding area, and the nearest teammate's chances of shutting down play. A fast support player can stay relatively close to the teammate attacking the player with the ball, to have a better chance of getting in there quickly if the teammate is outplayed. Equally, if the

The Ajax player Litmanen is under pressure from an opponent who also has a support player nearby.

opponent is fast and good at dribbling, the support player should maintain a fair distance from the teammate/opponent. When the area is crowded with opponents and teammates, it is usually best to remain a fair distance away from the teammate who is coming to meet the player in possession. This is partly because other team members can intervene if the teammate is outplayed, partly to be able to support if the ball is moved quickly, and partly to avoid being passed. The support player can also increase the distance between himself or herself and the teammates/opponent if the teammates have a good chance of winning the ball, thus hindering the opposition's forward play.

Position on the Pitch

The support player's position in relation to the teammate/opponent depends on where on the pitch the action is. In the opposition's half of the pitch, the support player can stand relatively close to the team member who is attacking the player in possession. But in the defensive zone it is risky to stand too close to the teammate/opponent, since the player with the ball could move wide and have a free run toward the goal. However, the support player should stand close to the opponent/teammate around or inside the penalty area; otherwise, the player with the ball will have a chance to outplay the teammate and finish.

The Hindering Game

If the attacker outplays the teammate and there is no immediate chance of winning the ball, the support player should try to hinder play, enabling the teammate to retreat and support. A defender can hinder the opponent's moves by maintaining the distance between them and using position to try to guide the attacker away from the direction of the game.

Communication

The support player must coordinate and communicate with the team member who is attacking the player in possession. The teammate can use position to try to force the player with the ball in the direction of the support player, thereby limiting the area the support player needs to cover (see also chapter 3).

Recovery Fundamentals

When coaching the recovery principle, the following specifics are important to consider.

Straight to Position

An outplayed player often stands rooted to the spot or follows hot on the heels of the victorious player in the hope of quickly regaining the ball. It is usually best, however, for the player to head directly back to a position of support for a teammate.

The Hindering Game

Until the support player is in position, other team members should hinder play. They should avoid committing themselves by tackling and maintain a distance between themselves and their opponents to ensure that they cannot easily be outplayed.

Practices and Drills

The following is a range of practices for support and recovery. The first four drills can be used as warm-up exercises.

Pass and Dribble

Players

Two.

Description

Player 1 passes to 2, after which 1 overtakes 2, who waits for 1 and turns to dribble past 1 (see figure 2.3). Once 2 gets a short distance past 1, player 2 turns and passes back to 1. Player 1 plays 2, and so on.

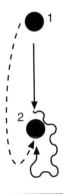

Figure 2.3   Pass and dribble.

Takeovers

Players

Three.

Description

Player 1 dribbles past 3, after which 2 takes over the ball. Player 1 continues running and stops short so that 2 can dribble past. See figure 2.4. After 2 has overtaken 1, 3 takes over the ball, 2 continues running, stops short, and so on.

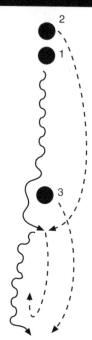

Figure 2.4 Takeovers.

Four-Player Support Drill

Players

Four.

Description

Player 1 passes to 2, who passes with the first touch to 3, who dribbles past first 2 and then 1, and finally 4. Player 3 then passes to 1, who passes with the first touch to 4, who dribbles past first 2, then 3, and finally 2. Player 4 passes to 2, and so on. See figure 2.5.

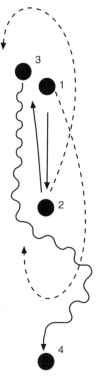

Figure 2.5 Four-player support drill.

Four-Square Drill

Pitch

20 square meters with four zones.

Players

Four versus four.

Description

One player from each team is in each of the four zones, as in figure 2.6. Players can pass the ball between the zones, but a player can only leave a zone by dribbling. A team scores points by dribbling into three zones in a row without the opposition gaining possession of the ball. When a player dribbles into a zone, the teammate in the zone cannot touch the ball and should move into the zone the player with the ball vacated.

Variation

The dribbling player, on entering a new zone, may pass to a teammate. If they lose the ball, one of them should move back to the recently vacated zone.

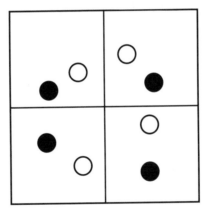

Figure 2.6   Four-square drill.

Hinder the Attacker

Pitch

Approximately one quarter of the pitch (an extended penalty area), divided into two zones (1 and 2) and one large goal.

Players

Four: one attacker (10), one defender (3), one support player (4), and a goalkeeper (1).

Description

Player 10 starts with the ball and should try to dribble past 3, who is only allowed in zone 2. Player 10 can only finish in zone 1. Player 4 is only allowed to defend in zone 1. See figure 2.7.

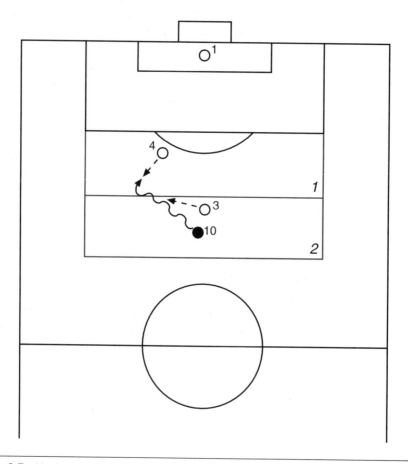

Figure 2.7 Hinder the attacker.

Scoring

As normal.

Variations

1. Player 4 starts 10 meters behind player 10. When 10 starts dribbling, 4 should start running toward the zone 1 penalty area and can only intervene there.
2. One more attacker (11) is added in zone 2. Only one of the attackers may dribble into zone 1.
3. Player 11 is restricted to zone 1. Both attackers may now be in zone 1 at the same time.
4. Player 3 may go into zone 1 when the ball has been played into it.

Coaching Points

Player 4 should try to intervene before 10 can finish; that is, 4 should remain relatively close to 10 and 3, but not so close that 10 can pass both 3 and 4 with a long run. You should highlight the coordination between the two defenders.

In variation one, 4 (the support player) should become accustomed to running into a recovery position before intervening. At the same time, 3 should try to keep 10 busy (hindering) until 4 is in position.

During variation two, 4 has to support 3 as well as keep one eye on the free attacker. This increases the pressure on the support player and provides further opportunities for highlighting the cooperation between the two defenders.

Variation three illustrates how a marking player (4) should get positioned to be able to support a teammate, and when 4 should stop marking and support.

In variation four, you can place further emphasis on the ways in which 4, once 3 has been outplayed, can hinder play to enable 3 to get back into the game.

This drill can also be developed in different areas of the pitch—for example, along the sidelines, where the attacker, after outplaying the defenders, can put a pass in to a teammate in the penalty area.

Keywords for Support

Positioning • Distance • Position on the pitch • Hinder • Communication

Keywords for Recovery

Direct • Hinder

Offensive Penetration

Pitch

Approximately two fifths of the pitch (extended penalty area), divided into three zones (1-3) and one large goal.

Players

Seven: one "server" (7), two attackers (10 and 11), two defenders (2 and 3), one support player (4), and a goalkeeper (1).

Description

Player 7 passes to either 10 or 11, who can then use 7 in a one-two (i.e., first-touch passes). See figure 2.8. Players 10 and 11 should play to each other (possibly using 7) until one of them can dribble into zone 1 and finish. Players may only shoot in zone 1.

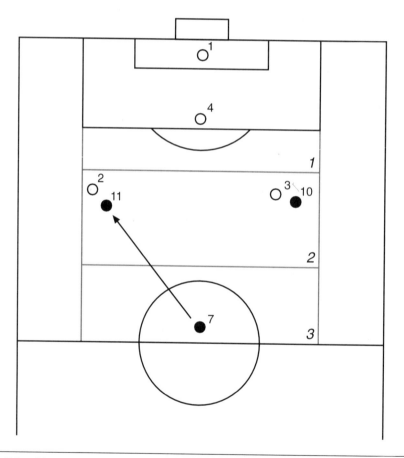

Figure 2.8   Offensive penetration.

Conditions

Player 4 must remain in zone 1, while 2 and 3 are restricted to zone 2; players 10 and 11 are allowed in zones 1 and 2 (however, only one of them may be in zone 1 at any one time), and 7 should keep to zone 3.

Scoring

As normal.

Variations

1. The ball can be passed into zone 1.
2. Zone 1 is extended lengthwise.
3. Another attacker is introduced. However, as before, only one attacker at a time may be in, or dribble into, zone 1.

Coaching Points

This exercise is a development of the Hinder the Attacker drill (see coaching points, page 41), in which the situation becomes more complex for the support player (4).

Variation one complicates 4's decisions in that 4 also needs to cover the areas into which the ball might be played.

In variation two, the area 4 has to cover is extended, making the task yet more difficult.

Variation three stretches 4's overview skills as well as the coordination between 2 and 3. You can stress the communication between 2, 3, and 4.

Keywords for Support

Positioning • Distance • Position on the pitch • Hinder • Communication

Keywords for Recovery

Direct • Hinder

Target Penetration

Pitch

Approximately one eighth of the pitch, divided into three zones (1-3) with seven goals (cones) placed on each baseline. See figure 2.9.

Players

Six: three versus three, of which one person on each team is a support player (white 3 and black 8).

Description

Normal game.

Conditions

Players 3 and 8 must remain in zones 1 and 3, respectively. No teammates and only one opponent may enter zones 1 and 3.

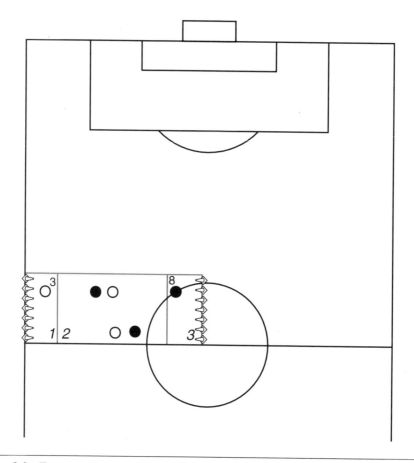

Figure 2.9 Target penetration.

Scoring

Teams score by hitting cones positioned on the baselines of zones 1 and 3.

Variations

1. White 3 and black 8 may also go into zone 2, but as soon as the white or black team loses the ball they must move back into their respective defensive zones.
2. Each team scores in one small goal instead of hitting the cones.

Coaching Points

This exercise focuses on the positions of 3 and 8 relative to their teammates and the player with the ball. It also gives the other players practice in judging when they can help the support player while ensuring that their direct opponent does not get the ball. And you can highlight the best time to attempt to win the ball—namely, when the opponent's area of operation is as small as possible.

In variation one, the situation gets more complicated for 3 and 8 in that they must also practice moving back to safeguard teammates. Their teammates should try to hinder play until their recovery player is in position.

In variation two, 3 and 8 should become accustomed to positioning themselves relative to the ball.

Keywords for Support

Positioning • Distance • Position on the pitch • Hinder • Communication

Keywords for Recovery

Direct • Hinder

Width and Transition Training

Pitch

Approximately one eighth of the pitch, divided into four zones (1-4) and a center zone. Two small goals are placed on the baselines of zones 1 and 4.

Players

Ten: five versus five, of whom one player (5) on each team is the support player.

Organization

The ball starts in zone 3. Two players from each team are in zones 2 and 3, while black 5 and white 5 are positioned in zones 1 and 4, respectively. See figure 2.10.

Description

Normal game. Each team defends and attacks two small goals.

Conditions

Black 5 and white 5 must remain in zones 1 and 4 respectively. No players may enter the center zone. When the ball is in zones 2 and 3, all players should revert to their original zones.

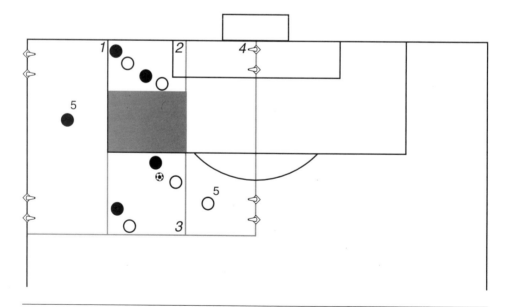

Figure 2.10 Width and transition training.

Scoring

The teams score in the opposition's two small goals.

Variations

1. The number 5 players may move freely over the pitch, but when their teams lose the ball they must move back into their respective defensive zones. They may go into the center zone.
2. All players may pass through the center zone, but no one can touch the ball there.

Coaching Points

See coaching points for Hinder the Attacker (page 41) and Offensive Penetration (page 43).

In variation one, the emphasis is on cooperation between the support players (the number 5s) and their teammates. The number 5s should quickly move back to safeguard their teammates, while other team members should hinder play so that the 5s can get back into position. Variation one will also increase the chances of breakthroughs—and of 5's intervention, since this player is an extra in the team's attack. You can influence the number of breakthroughs by altering the length and breadth of the center zone.

The game becomes more complex in variation two, approaching the true game situation.

Keywords for Support

Positioning • Distance • Position on the pitch • Hinder • Communication

Keywords for Recovery

Direct • Hinder

Speedy Retreat

Pitch

Approximately one quarter of the pitch, divided into four zones (1-4). Three goals (cones) are placed on the baselines of zones 1 and 4.

Players

Twelve: six versus six, of which two players from each team are support/recovery players (5 and 6).

Description

Normal game. Each team defends and attacks the goals. When a team loses the ball, the number 5 and 6 players on that team should change zones. "Losing the ball" is defined as being when the opposition passes the ball successfully within the team. The ball may not be played into the attacking zones (1 and 4) from a team's own half of the pitch—that is, from zones 3 and 2 respectively. See figure 2.11.

Conditions

Players 5 and 6 must remain in either zone 1 or zone 4. They may not touch the ball in zones 2 and 3. The players in zones 2 and 3 are also restricted to these zones.

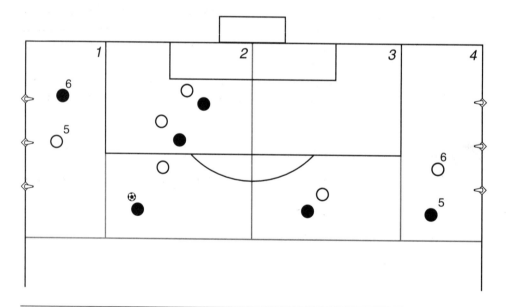

Figure 2.11 Speedy retreat.

Scoring

Teams score by hitting the opposition's cones.

Variations

1. A team may play the ball from its own half into the attacking zone (1 or 4).
2. The number 5 and 6 players may attempt to win the ball between zones 1 and 4. If they succeed, the ball is put forward into the new zone.
3. The number 5 and 6 players may move freely over the pitch.

Coaching Points

This practice focuses on speedy retreats on the part of the recovery players when the ball is lost. In addition, it highlights the ways other team members can hinder the game—avoiding committing themselves to tackles, for example, and maintaining an appropriate distance so that they cannot be put out of play. Hindering the game should preferably take place in the opposition's half of the pitch so the opposing team cannot pass to the free attackers in the attacking zone.

In variation one, it becomes more important for the recovery player to run back quickly.

In variation two, the recovery player should gain an understanding of what it means to get into a recovery position quickly. Players might sometimes be in a position to win the ball, but, on the other hand, if they are unsuccessful and the ball is played forward to the free attackers, this might cost them.

Variation three puts the recovery players in situations where they need to judge to what degree they should participate in the game or retreat and support.

Keywords for Support

Positioning • Distance • Position on the pitch • Hinder • Communication

Keywords for Recovery

Direct • Hinder

Short Passes

Pitch

The penalty area, divided into 4 zones (1-4). Four goals (cones) are placed on the baselines in zones 1 and 4.

Players

Eight: four versus four.

Organization

Each team member has a separate zone. See figure 2.12.

Description

Normal game. The ball cannot be played across two zones. The player with the ball can either pass to the player in the next zone or dribble into the next zone. If the player dribbles into the next zone, the teammate there should immediately move back to the zone the player with the ball came from.

Conditions

Each team should always have one player in each zone, but for short periods the team in possession may have two players in one zone.

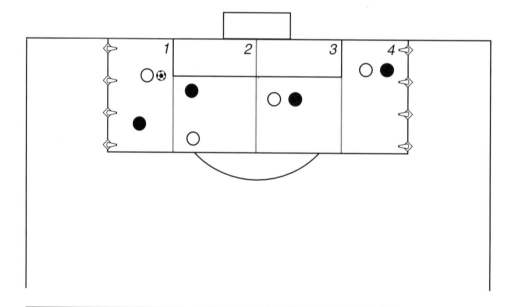

Figure 2.12 Short passes.

Scoring

The teams score by hitting one of the opposition's cones.

Variations

1. The ball can be played across several zones.
2. Each team scores in a two-meter-wide goal instead of hitting the cones.

Coaching Points

This exercise focuses on the issues involved in leaving a direct opponent (who should be marked) to support a teammate. It likewise highlights how an opponent should be marked when a player needs to support a teammate (see also the discussion of covering and marking in chapter 1).

In variation one, you should emphasize that defenders who are not close to the ball must mark their opponents closely.

In variation two, the support players should become used to keeping the location of their own goal in mind.

Keywords for Support

Positioning • Distance • Position on the pitch • Hinder • Communication

Keywords for Recovery

Direct • Hinder

Support Intervention

Pitch

Approximately one eighth of the pitch, divided into five zones (1-5).

Players

Eight: four versus four.

Organization

Two players (center zone players) from each team are in the center zone (4), while the other two players (outer zone players) from each team position themselves in the diametrically opposite outer zones (1/5 and 2/3). See figure 2.13. After a set length of time, the center zone players switch with the outer zone players.

Description

A center zone player can only leave zone 4 by dribbling into one of the opposition's outer zones. The teams score points by passing from one of the opposition's outer zones to one of their own outer zones. When the outer zone players win or receive the ball, they may not be attacked, and they should pass to a teammate in the center zone. The player who was originally in the center zone runs back to the center zone.

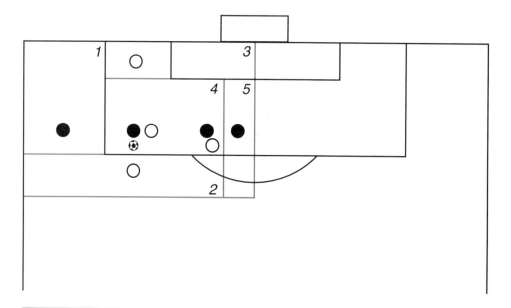

Figure 2.13 Support intervention.

Scoring

See previous section.

Variations

1. The players in the center zone can use their outer zone players in one-twos (i.e., the ball is passed back first time).
2. Each team may have one of its outer zone players in the center zone (4).
3. All the outer zone players may go into the center zone.

Coaching Points

The players in the outer zones are the support players. They should become accustomed to intervening when their teammates have been outplayed or passed.

These players must intervene quickly, as the player dribbling into the zone has two passing options (2 outer zones). This exercise also hones the ability of the outer zone players to switch quickly from defense to attack, and vice versa.

Variation one tests the ability of the outer zone players to switch from defense to attack.

In variations two and three, you can concentrate on the role of the outer zone players as recovery players, since they are sometimes "forced" back in their zones to help defend shots on goal.

Keywords for Support

Positioning • Distance • Position on the pitch • Hinder • Communication

Keywords for Recovery

Direct • Hinder

CHAPTER 3

Forcing the Opponent's Direction

Another defensive principle is the forcing of the opponent's direction. A defender can use positioning to increase the probability of an opponent dribbling or passing in a certain direction. The attackers are "forced" toward areas where the playing options are limited or toward other defenders who can then intervene (setting a trap).

A team can apply the principle of pressuring an opponent in a certain direction anywhere on the pitch, but it's particularly useful when the player with the ball is close to the sideline or baseline (see figure 3.1a). The principle can be used both by one defender and by the team as a whole.

A defending team can use the position of players to minimize the opposition's attacking area and, to some extent, to control their upfield play. If players cover a particular area, they can force the player with the ball to pass to an area that might benefit the defending team (see figure 3.1b). This might be an area where, should the opposition lose the ball, the defenders could initiate a dangerous counterattack, or where the opponent is "forced" to pass to a player who is not so good at holding onto the ball. Figure 3.2 demonstrates how the whole team can work together to control the upfield play of the opposition. The black team "tempts" the opposition to attack through the center by opening it up. After the opposition has put the ball into the desired area, the black team attacks inward from all sides, thereby increasing its chances of winning the ball.

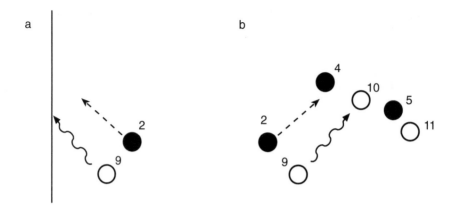

Figure 3.1   (a) Player 2's positioning forces 9 toward the sideline. (b) Player 2 forces 9 to dribble in the direction of 10; 9 could then be attacked by 4 or 5.

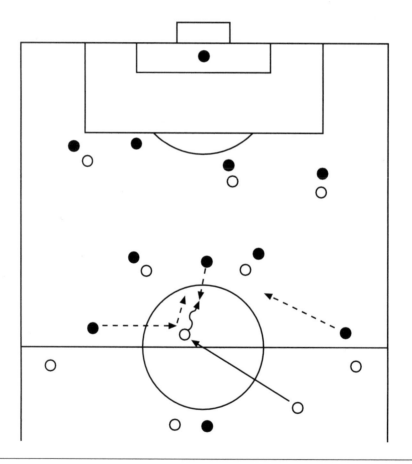

Figure 3.2   The black team opens up the center until the opposition plays the ball there, then they attack inward from all sides.

Once a defender has forced the opponent out to the sidelines, a physical tackle will often win the ball.

Goals

- To force an opponent in a direction in which it is difficult to work constructively or where there is a good chance of losing the ball.
- To force the player with the ball to pass to a teammate who is less likely to keep the ball (the team's weak link) or who is in an unfavorable position.

Forcing Direction Fundamentals

Following are the main points defenders should consider when using the tactic of forcing the opponent's direction.

Distance

The distance between the defender and the player with the ball depends on the speed of the players and the dribbling skills of the player in possession. If the defender is quicker than the player with the ball, the distance between them can be short; it should be greater if the defender is relatively slow and the attacker is good at dribbling the ball.

The distance also depends on how much the player wants the attacker to take the ball in a certain direction. The closer the defender is to the attacker, the more probable it becomes that the attacker will run in the desired direction. This increases the risk, however, of the attacker managing to dribble past the defender.

Positioning

The defender's position relative to the player with the ball depends on teamwork—how good the support is. A defender with support can stay more by the side of the opponent and concentrate on winning the ball.

Coordination

Deliberately pressuring an opponent to move in the direction of teammates requires close coordination between the defenders involved. Players who are farthest back down the pitch should make their positions known to their teammate who is coming to meet the player with the ball. This gives the defending player a better chance of judging the direction to pressure the player with the ball.

Open/Close

The players can use their positions, relative to their opponents, to first open an area, making it attractive to opponents, and then close it when the ball has been played into the area, attacking the player with the ball and blocking playing options.

Practices and Drills

Following is a range of useful practices for coaching the principle of determining the opposition's direction. The first two drills are effective as warm-up exercises.

One-on-One Force Out

Players

Two: one attacker (1) and one defender (2).

Organization

Player 1 stands between two lines about 15 meters apart.

Description

Player 1 dribbles toward 2, who should force 1 out over the sideline.
Player 1 should try to dribble over the baseline. See figure 3.3.

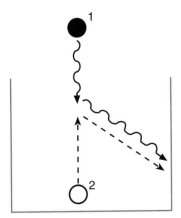

Figure 3.3   One-on-one force out.

Shepherding the Takeover

Players

Six: four attackers (1-4) and two defenders (5 and 6).

Organization

The attackers form a triangle with two in the corner by the ball. One defender (5) takes a position near the ball while the other (6) gets in position near 3.

Description

Player 1 dribbles toward 2 while 5 follows passively. Player 2 takes over the ball and 5 should try to direct the attacker toward the corner with 6, who takes over the marking. If this is not successful, 5 must take another turn. The attacking players should "put up" with being "sent" in a certain direction only if the defender's position is appropriate. See figure 3.4.

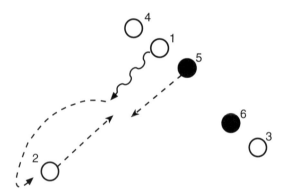

Figure 3.4 Shepherding the takeover.

Shepherding the Attacker

Pitch

Approximately one quarter of the pitch, consisting of an extended penalty area (zones 1 and 2) and a large goal.

Players

Four: one server (7), one striker (10), one defender (3), and a goalkeeper (1).

Description

Player 7 passes to 10, who dribbles down toward 3, as in figure 3.5a. Player 7 indicates with an arm motion the direction in which 3 should try to force 10.

Conditions

Player 3 is only allowed in zone 2, while 10 can go into zones 1 and 2. Player 7 should be outside zones 1 and 2.

Scoring

As normal.

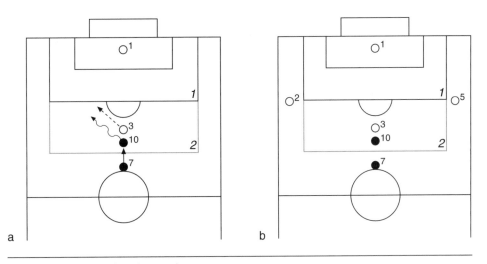

a   b

Figure 3.5 Shepherding the attacker.

Variations

1. Player 7 can be used as 10's teammate.
2. Two more defenders (2 and 5) are positioned in the corners of the penalty area (see figure 3.5b). Players 2 and 5 can only intervene as defenders if they are on the side 7 indicates, and if 10 dribbles to that side. Players 2 and 5 may only take part in the game immediately in front of the penalty area.
3. Another attacker (11) joins in, starting about 10 meters behind 7. Player 11 should run in the opposite direction to that indicated by 7. The ball cannot be played backward.

Coaching Points

Player 3 should first become accustomed to taking up a position that forces 10 in the appropriate direction. Then 3 should get positioned in such a way that intervention is possible before 10 has a chance to finish.

Variation one presents another opportunity to focus on 3's positioning in relation to 10 in that 3 has to be aware of yet another direction of play.

In variation two, 3 will get some idea of the importance of forcing 10 to the correct side—the side where 3 can obtain support. Player 3 should also understand that it can be a good idea to force 10 in a certain direction without active intervention on his own part.

Variation three increases the need for 3's positioning skills, because 3 has to prevent 10 from passing to 11.

Keywords for Defenders

Distance • Positioning • Coordination • Open/close

Ball Recovery

Pitch

One half of the penalty area.

Players

Eight: the players are divided into pairs.

Organization

All players except one pair have a ball, as shown in figure 3.6.

Description

The pair without a ball should try to win one. If a pair loses a ball, they should then try to win one.

Conditions

If a player dribbles outside the area, the player and his partner become ball winners.

Scoring

None.

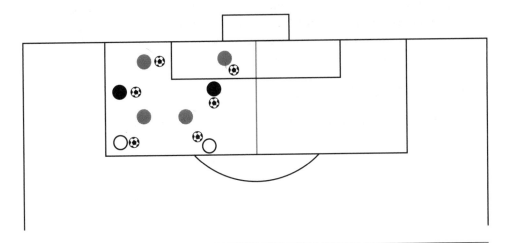

Figure 3.6 Ball recovery.

Variations

1. Only one ball is allowed per pair of players—and one in the two-player team must be in possession of it.
2. The players are no longer in pairs. There are always two ball winners. A player who loses the ball also becomes a ball winner, so the number of ball winners increases every time a ball is won.

Coaching Points

The ball winners should try to force a player with a ball toward the boundaries of the area or toward other players/their teammates so they can win the ball more easily. During this game, you may wish to highlight the positioning of the ball winner relative to the player with the ball, as well as the necessary coordination between the ball winners.

Variation one concentrates on coordination between the ball winners, since it becomes more difficult to win a ball. One ball winner can cover a pass to a teammate while the player with the ball is "forced" across toward the other ball winner or the boundary.

In variation two, the number of ball winners increases constantly, offering further chances for focusing on their coordination. The challenge, "Who can maintain possession of the ball the longest?" may motivate the players competitively.

Keywords for Defenders

Distance • Positioning • Coordination • Open/close

Soccer Sharks and Minnows

Pitch

Approximately one fifth of the pitch, consisting of an extended penalty area divided into four zones (1-4).

Players

Six: three teams of two players.

Organization

One team attacks while the other two defend. Each player on the two defending teams covers a zone (see figure 3.7). The two players on the attacking team each start with a ball by their respective baselines. The teams rotate after each attack.

Description

The players on the attacking team have 30 seconds to dribble from one baseline to the other.

Conditions

The players on the attacking team cannot be in the same zone. If a defender wins the ball, the attacker cannot continue. Once across the edge of the penalty box, the attacker cannot change zones.

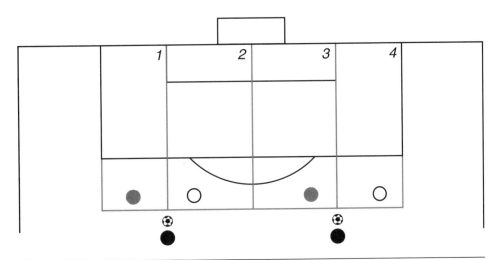

Figure 3.7 Soccer sharks and minnows.

Scoring

If a player on the attacking team succeeds in dribbling from one baseline to the other within the set time, the attacking team gets one point. The defending team responsible for the relevant zone loses one point.

Variations

1. The players on the two defending teams are positioned side by side.
2. The zones are extended.
3. The attacking team has only one ball.

Coaching Points

In this exercise, the defending players should try to nudge an attacker into a zone covered by a defender from a competing team, or, if the attacker is in the penalty area near the edge of the zone, so that the defender can try to win the ball. You can thus highlight the positioning of the defenders in relation to the attackers.

In variation one, the defenders should understand the importance of coordinating with their teammates. The increased size of the zones makes their task of defending more difficult, providing another opportunity to focus on the demands placed on the defenders.

In variation three, you can highlight how a teammate of the player pressuring the attacker should get in position. A defender who gambles on reaching the ball if it is passed or who follows the teammate closely risks the ball being played behind him or her. Rather, the defender should stand close by the opponent to intervene quickly if the player receives the ball.

Keywords for Defenders

Distance • Positioning • Coordination • Open/close

Defender Awareness Game

Pitch

A penalty area, divided into four zones.

Players

Six: four attackers (black team) and two defenders (white team).

Organization

Two attackers each are positioned in zones 1 and 4, and the two defenders are positioned in zones 2 and 3. One of the attackers in zone 1 starts with a ball.

Description

The attacking players dribble into zones 2 or 3 and should try to pass to one of the two attackers in the opposite zone (1 or 4). See figure 3.8.

Conditions

The two defenders should remain in their zones. The attacking players may not dribble into zones 1 or 4, and only one attacker may be in zones 2 and 3 at any one time.

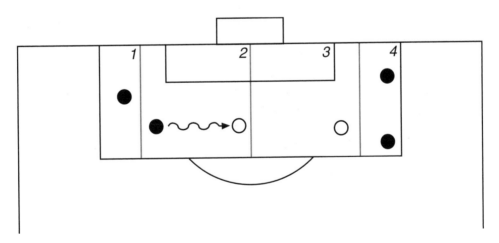

Figure 3.8 Defender awareness game.

Scoring

The attackers score one point when they pass the ball successfully from one of the central zones (2 or 3) to one of the attackers in the zone opposite their original zone (1 or 4).

Variations

1. The attacker who receives the ball dribbles into the central zone.
2. The attackers can only dribble forward.
3. An attacker who loses the ball becomes a defender. No points are awarded in this variation.
4. A pass should come from the central zone opposite the one into which the attacker first dribbled—that is, the attacker should dribble through the first central zone.

Coaching Points

The defender who first meets the player with the ball should try to block a long pass while preventing the attacker from dribbling past. The defender should also "force" the attacker who is dribbling the ball toward the other central zone defender, so that the other defender can intervene successfully. The first defender should therefore be close to the attacker while remaining aware of the other defender's position.

Variation one presents opportunities for several different starting positions and increases the pressure on the defenders to quickly realign.

In variation two the situation is made more difficult for the attackers, and the defenders should concentrate on reducing the attacking directions. This enables you to focus on positioning the defenders in relation to the player with the ball.

You can introduce variation three to shake things up a little. It can be a way of increasing the motivation of the attackers.

In variation four, you should pay special attention to the coordination between the two defenders. You can use this variation if the attacking players are tending to use long passes.

Keywords for Defenders

Distance • Positioning • Coordination • Open/close

Trap the Attackers

Pitch

One half of the pitch, with two zones (1 and 2) and three small goals on each sideline.

Players

Twelve: six versus six.

Description

As normal, with the teams defending and attacking three small goals. See figure 3.9.

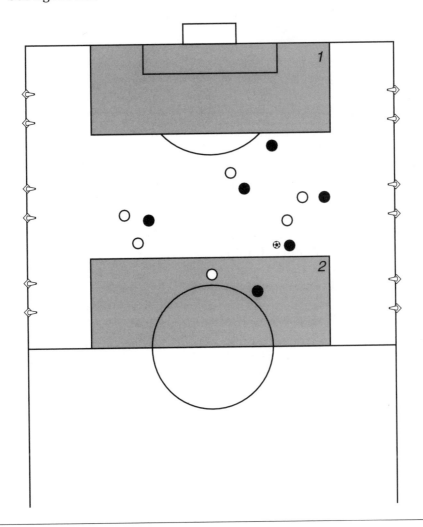

Figure 3.9 Trap the attackers.

Conditions

In zones 1 and 2, the players may have no more than two touches on the ball.

Scoring

Goals are scored in one of the opposition's three small goals.

Variations

1. If the ball is not in either of the zones, only the defending team may have players in zones 1 and 2.
2. The defending team should have at least one player in each zone.
3. The defending team may have players in zones 1 and 2 only if the attacking team has a player there.
4. The ball cannot be passed from zones 1 and 2.

Coaching Points

The defending team's players should try to pressure their opponents out into zones 1 and 2 to make the task of attacking more difficult. The players should understand, through this, the effects of forcing an opponent in a certain direction. During the game, you can also focus on the importance of closing the "trap"—that the coordination between the teammate meeting the player with the ball and the other players actually works.

This last issue is even more important in variations one and two. In variation two, the teammates in zones 1 and 2 can only be used if the team succeeds in getting opponents to play or dribble the ball into one of these zones.

Variation four can give the players a clear idea of the advantages of moving the opposition into certain areas of the pitch.

Keywords for Defenders

Distance • Positioning • Coordination • Open/close

CHAPTER 4

Organization of Cover

Chapters 1 through 3 describe individual defensive actions and principles involving only a few players. The next seven chapters will focus on team tactics in the defensive game.

Soccer is a constant switch between "we have the ball" and "they have the ball." Figure 4.1 illustrates how the attacking and defensive games consist of different phases that depend on where the ball is on the pitch. The defending team should try to hinder the opposition's upfield play, win the ball, and prevent a breakthrough or shot in its own defensive zone. This can be done at various times and in various ways. Each team develops its own way of defending. Defensive tactics involve choosing a team strategy that exploits player strengths so that the team can win the ball and prevent the opposition from breaking through and scoring.

Each individual on the defending team should think along defensive lines: "How can I help my team to win back the ball?" The player should also think about how to turn position to attack advantage when the team regains the ball. The contributions of the individual should be coordinated with those of teammates in order to create efficient defensive play. The book *Soccer Systems & Strategies* describes different types of defensive games, and this chapter explores them more deeply.

There are two main principles in the organization of a team's defense when the opposition has the ball:

- Man-to-man cover, in which each player covers a particular opponent
- Zonal cover, in which each player covers a set area of the pitch

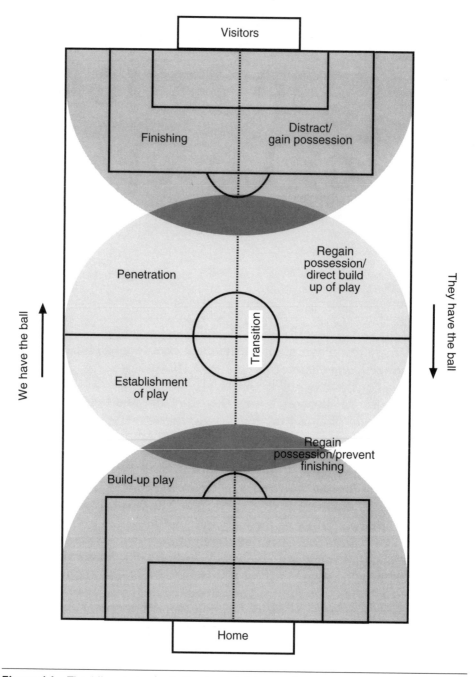

Figure 4.1   The different phases of offensive and defensive play.

Figure 4.2 provides an overview of the covering principles and their specific forms. Man-to-man cover can be used with either zonal or player marking, as can zonal cover.

Combination defenses use a combination of zonal and man-to-man cover, sometimes marking one of the opposing players exhaustively (point cover). Chapter 7 explains combination defense in more detail.

A team will usually employ one of four specific defensive formats within zonal and man-to-man cover. These four formats will be described in detail later in this chapter, but they are briefly summarized in the next section using true game situations.

The white team has won the ball from the black team and is playing upfield from its own half of the pitch. The players on the black team now have a choice of actions, depending on the form of cover they are using.

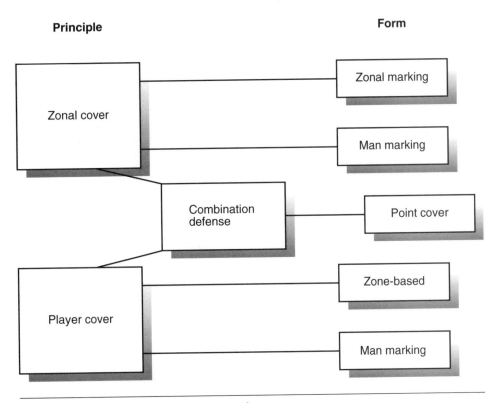

Figure 4.2 The covering principles and their forms.

The Norwegian national team always uses zonal marking. When the player in possession comes into a zone, the defender responsible applies intense pressure to the opponent—in this case, Danish player Brian Laudrup. The other players should move toward this zone and be ready to take on the player with the ball should he move into their areas.

Man-to-Man Cover With Zonal Marking

The defender takes position in a certain area of the pitch and, throughout the game situation, marks the opponent who is in this area when the opposing team has crossed the centerline. When the game situation has been dealt with through, say, the ball being won back or a dead ball situation, the defender returns to that area. See figure 4.3.

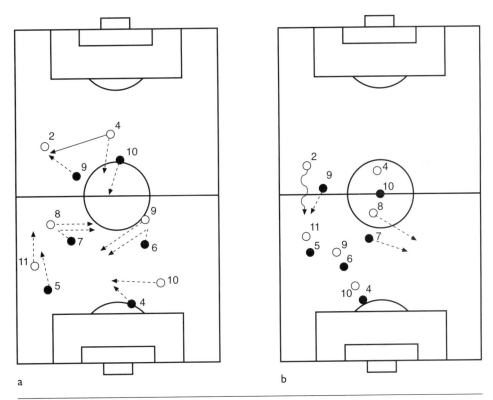

a   b

Figure 4.3   (a) Black 7 follows white 8 within his area and marks him. (b) 7 continues to mark 8 and 6 continues to mark white 9, even if 8 and 9 switch areas.

Man-to-Man Cover With Player Marking

The defender follows a particular opponent and marks this player in all defensive situations throughout the game. See figure 4.4.

Zonal Cover With Zonal Marking

The defender takes position in a set area of the pitch and makes moves linked only to those of teammates. If an opponent enters this area, the

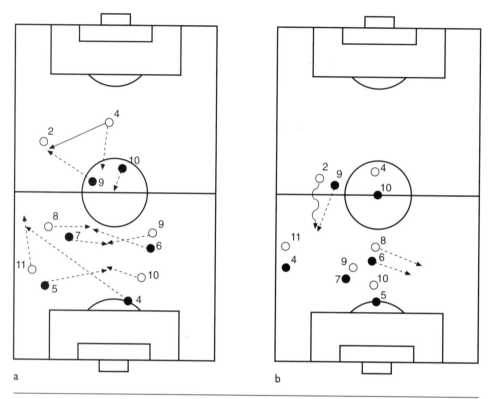

Figure 4.4 Player 7 follows his direct opponent (9) throughout the defensive phase.

defender takes up a position that allows for both following the movements of teammates and being ready to mark the opponent if necessary. See figure 4.5.

Zonal Cover With Player Marking

The defender takes position in a set area of the pitch and makes moves linked to those of the closest opponent. The nearer the opponent is to the ball, the closer the marking. If the opponent leaves the area, a teammate takes over marking and the player takes over marking the teammate's opponent. See figure 4.6. Table 4.1 on page 79 describes the advantages and disadvantages of zonal and man-to-man cover.

Until the middle of the 1970s, there was a clear distinction between teams who played with zonal cover and those using man-to-man cover. During the last 10 to 15 years, these ideas have become blurred, until today there is some confusion about what they actually mean. The Danish Soccer League Statistics Group at the 1996 European Championships remarked in its analysis that the tournament displayed great variation and diversity in the ways defensive games were organized, and that, following these

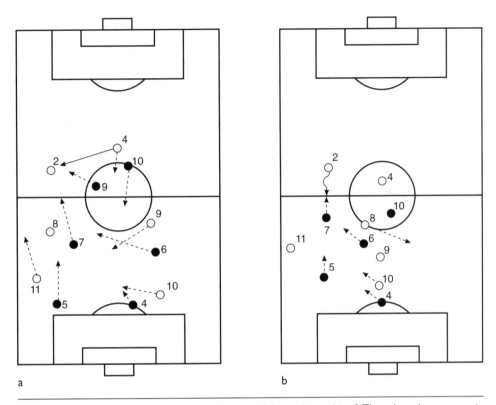

Figure 4.5   (a) Player 7 makes moves in his area while marking white 8. The other players move in relation to the ball; 7 pays attention to the opposition. (b) 7 moves in relation to the ball and teammates without focusing on 7.

European Championships, the definitions of zonal and man-to-man cover were blurring and changing. The UEFA Technical Committee's report categorized the defensive organization of the 16 participating countries according to the importance the team placed on the principles of zonal or man-to-man cover. This analysis demonstrated an even distribution between the two formats. It was primarily the teams from western and southern Europe who based their game on zonal cover, while teams from central and eastern Europe in particular stuck to man-to-man cover. At the 1998 World Cup and 2000 European Championship, more teams used zonal cover.

Choice of Defensive Organization

Zonal and man-to-man cover are such different methods of organizing a defense that you cannot simply change the format from one game to the next. The distribution and requirements of roles for the two formats are extremely different.

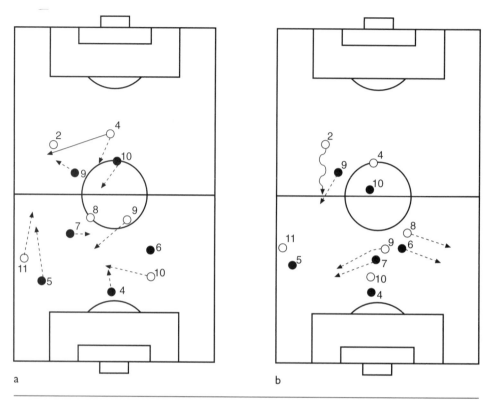

Figure 4.6 (a) 7 follows and marks 8 in his area. (b) 7 and 6 switch marking, since 8 and 9 switch areas.

When you take over a new team, you should first focus on the team's existing defensive organization. Does the player material tally with the quality of the defensive work, or can the team's defensive ability be improved by altering its defensive organization? Bearing in mind what you know of the player material, you should carry out this analysis while weighing the advantages and disadvantages of the two organizational formats, as described earlier. You should, among other things, assess the ability of the central players to contribute in important game situations. For example, can the blocker cope out on the wing? Can the back take part in a quick counterattack if in midfield—or should the blocker participate in this case? Can the fullback get back quickly enough to cover a winger? If the results of analysis suggest a change in defensive organization, there must be time available to implement it. A change in the defensive game will require at least a month's training for a professional team and substantially longer for other teams.

Chapter 4 of *Soccer Systems & Strategies* provides some guidelines for training players' tactical abilities and developing a team into a powerful attacking unit. It is particularly important for you to alternate between training the players in small groups and as a full team while the team is learning a tactical defensive principle.

Table 4.1 Advantages and Disadvantages of Man-to-Man and Zonal Cover

Man-to-man cover

Advantages	Disadvantages
Clear responsibility for players	The defender can be drawn away from the central area
Easy to practice	
Always close cover in the area around the ball	Confusion can arise regarding cover
	Free areas may be created in the defensive zone
Can exploit the strength of defenders	
	Difficult to help other defenders
	Physically demanding
	Uncomfortable when participating in attacking play
	The players can be in inappropriate positions when the ball is won

Zonal cover

Advantages	Disadvantages
Clear defensive position	Uncertainty regarding responsibilities
No free areas	Long period of training
Optimal positioning of players when the ball is won	Fear of leaving the area, thereby limiting the participation of players in attacking play
Many passing options once the ball is won	

The next chapter explains man-to-man cover in detail. Chapter 6 discusses zonal cover. Combination defense is in chapter 7. One thing common to the two primary covering principles is that they are carried out using the general principles of defensive organization. These principles focus on how a team creates depth in defensive play and how to coordinate the sections of players (see chapters 8 and 9, respectively).

In zonal cover with player marking, situations occasionally arise where opponents are not tightly covered. Note how Zidane's opponent, in the center of the picture, is following his break.

CHAPTER 5

Man-to-Man Cover

The main principle of man-to-man cover is that a player covers one of the opposing players throughout a defensive situation (see figure 5.1 on page 82). As discussed earlier, there are two types of man-to-man cover (also known as player cover):

- Man-to-man cover with player marking: each player on the team covers a particular opponent throughout the game.
- Zone-based man-to-man cover: on losing the ball, defenders mark the closest opponent until the team regains the ball.

German soccer has employed man-to-man cover for many years, and with substantial success. In recent times, however, the German national team has abandoned this type of cover, increasing the freedom of the defenders. At the 1996 European Championships, the German national team was one of the most frequent users of their defenders, such as Sammer and Ziege, in attacking play.

Some elite-level teams always use man-to-man cover. For example, the Czech national team had great success with zone-based man-to-man cover at the 1996 European Championships. The Czechs also proved that player cover is tiring. Several of the Czech players were physically exhausted toward the end of the games and had to be substituted or play at a lower rate.

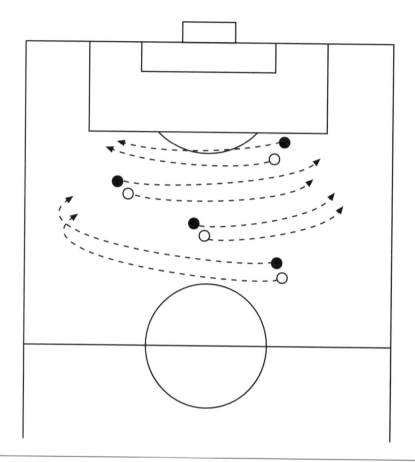

Figure 5.1 In man-to-man cover, a player covers his opponent throughout a defensive situation.

This form of cover can be used to advantage by all or part of a team that is not interacting properly, because it is clear for the players. Starting with man-to-man cover, you can gradually develop a more all-around form of cover, for example, by allowing first the attackers and then the midfielders to use zonal cover (see also combination defense, in chapter 7).

Goals

- A clear, simple defensive formation.
- Opponents to be tightly marked.

Man-to-Man Cover Fundamentals

In man-to-man cover, there are several issues players should be aware of regardless of whether the marking is to be player marking or zone-based.

Since enjoying success in the 1996 European Championships, the Czech Republic has employed zonal-based player cover. Kadlec, for example, usually covered Ebbe Sand during the 1998 friendly between the Czech Republic and Denmark.

Seeking the Opponent

As soon as the ball is lost, players should move toward their direct opponents. If the team uses a "waiting" style of defense, players should move back down the pitch and await their direct opponents.

Marking

Marking (including the distance between the defender and the direct opponent) follows the general principles for cover. For further information, see chapter 1.

Break Out

If a team member is outplayed or passed, the closest teammate should break out from man-to-man cover and try to cover the free opponent. Alternatively, the sweeper can cover the opponent (see the following section). A defender breaking out calls to teammates, who should take up positions enabling them to back up. When the outplayed player gets back into position, the players return to their direct opponents.

Sweeper

If a teammate is outplayed in the defender's half of the pitch, the sweeper can challenge the player with the ball. The sweeper's primary task is to hinder the forward movement of the player with the ball. The other players should be particularly vigilant on these occasions, and they should move away from their direct opponents when the player with the ball has a chance of moving directly toward the goal.

Return Runs

A player who has been outplayed should move back down the pitch—taking over a direct opponent from a teammate, if necessary.

Practices and Drills

You can use the following exercises for both player cover with man marking and zone-based player cover. When explaining them, you should highlight the type of cover the players are to use. The coaching points for the individual drills list any particular conditions to be aware of in using one or another form of cover. The first two drills should be used as warm-up exercises.

Marking Warm-Up

Players

Six.

Description

Player 1 dribbles forward with the ball, and 2 follows; player 3 runs forward and takes over the ball from 1 at around the halfway point, while 4 follows. When 1 has passed the ball on to 3, players 1 and 3 continue forward, while 2 and 4 follow. Player 5 runs forward to 3 and takes over the ball, while 6 follows 5. Player 5 dribbles forward and 1 takes over the ball. Players 5 and 1 run forward, with 6 and 2 running behind. Continue in this way; players 1, 3, and 5 should change with 2, 4, and 6 after a while. See figure 5.2.

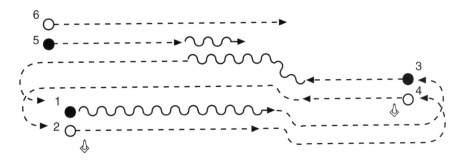

Figure 5.2 Marking warm-up.

Cover Practice

Pitch

The penalty area, with seven cones.

Players

Ten: five versus five.

Description

Normal game; a point is scored by hitting one of the cones. Players use player cover on each other in pairs. See figure 5.3. This game is physically demanding and should not be used at the beginning of a warm-up.

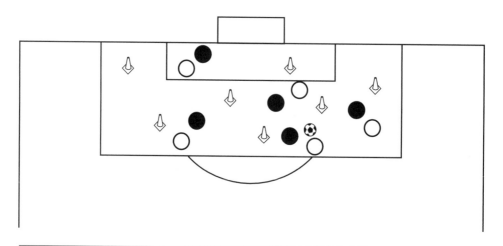

Figure 5.3 Cover practice.

Cover Zone

Pitch

Approximately one third of the pitch, divided into two zones (1 and 2) with a large goal.

Players

Six: a goalkeeper (1) and two defenders (3 and 4) on the black team, and two attackers (10 and 11) and a midfielder (8) on the white team.

Organization

All players start in zone 1 with the exception of 8, who should be in zone 2. Player 8 starts with the ball. See figure 5.4.

Description

Normal game.

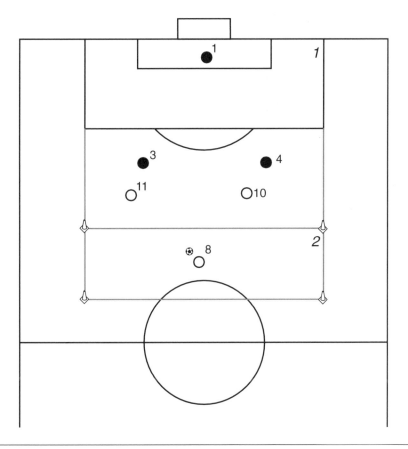

Figure 5.4 Cover zone.

Conditions

Players may not switch zones. A one meter offside rule is in effect—that is, the attackers must be more than one meter offside in order to be penalized. If the ball is won in zone 1, the black team should pass it to 8.

Scoring

The white team gains five points by scoring in the large goal. The black team scores one point by winning the ball, which is defined as being when two black-team players in a row touch it.

Variations

1. A sweeper (5) is introduced on the defending team.
2. A defender (6) is introduced to mark 8. Players 6 and 8 can both go into zones 1 and 2.
3. An extra attacker (7) is introduced. This player may go only into zone 2.
4. Player 7 may go into both zones 1 and 2.

Coaching Points

This exercise enables you to focus on the basic requirements of player cover. You can highlight the distance between 3 and 4 and their respective opponents, and you can emphasize the need to be prepared to break out if a teammate is outplayed. Players 3 and 4 should not to be tempted to intervene when the ball is passed to their teammate's marker.

Variation one focuses on the teamwork between 3 or 4 and 5. If either 3 or 4 is outplayed, the other should judge whether to leave the direct opponent or allow 5 to cover the free opponent.

Variation two limits the passing options for the white team, helping the defenders to concentrate on marking their direct opponents.

Variation three increases the pressure on the defenders. The situations become more complex, and the players must always be aware of the positions of both their direct opponents and the rest of the players.

In variation four, the pressure increases still further; you may wish to focus on the role of the sweeper (5) in player cover.

Keywords

Seek out opponent • Marking • Break out • Sweeper • Retreat

Cover Organization

Pitch

One half of the pitch, divided into two zones (1 and 2) with a large goal.

Players

Nine: four on the white team versus four and a goalkeeper on the black team, defending the large goal.

Organization

The black team starts in zone 1, the white team in zone 2, as shown in figure 5.5. The white team starts with the ball.

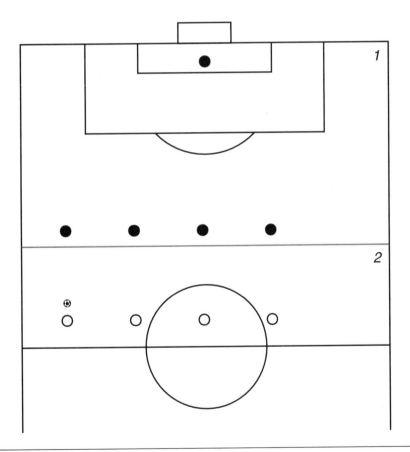

Figure 5.5   Cover organization.

Description

Normal game; when play halts, the white team starts again with the ball in zone 2. Black-team players should cover an opponent throughout the defensive phase.

Conditions

The black team's players must remain in zone 1. When the white team's players are in zone 1, they may not move back into zone 2 until the black team has won the ball or the white team has scored. A one-meter offside rule is applied, meaning the attackers must be more than one meter offside to be penalized.

Scoring

The white team scores five points by scoring in the large goal. The black team scores one point by playing the ball up into the center circle from zone 1.

Variations

1. There are no zonal divisions. The black team can attack the white team farther up the pitch.
2. Players have a maximum of 3 touches.
3. Players have at least 3 touches.
4. A sweeper joins the black team.

Coaching Points

When the white team's players move into zone 1, each player on the black team should quickly seek out an opponent. For player cover with player marking, each of the black team's players should be assigned a particular player to cover. In this type of cover, the defenders should always move to be ready to meet their direct opponents as soon as the attackers enter zone 1. With area-based player cover, the black team's players should maintain their positions relative to one another until seeking out the first player who enters their respective areas. The defenders should then follow their direct opponents until the attacking phase is over. You should stress to the players the importance of tightly marking their direct opponents if they are near the ball, and remind them that they should be ready to break out if a teammate is outplayed.

In variation one, the defenders must decide when to attack the players on the white team.

Variation two increases the pressure on the attackers to move in accordance with their teammates, which will likewise force the defenders to move.

In variation three, the defenders know that the attackers will keep the ball, and this should give them an idea of how important it is to remain close to a direct opponent.

In variation four, players should become accustomed to judging when they should break out and when they should allow the sweeper to take over in the event of a teammate being outplayed.

Keywords

Seek out opponent • Marking • Break out • Sweeper • Retreat

Player Cover

Pitch

Approximately one third of the pitch, with a centerline and four small goals on each half of the pitch, as shown in figure 5.6.

Players

Ten: five versus five.

Description

Normal game.

Conditions

Both teams should use player cover.

Scoring

Teams score by playing the ball through one of the opposition's four goals.

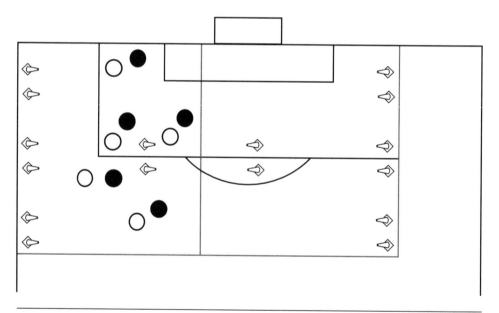

Figure 5.6 Player cover.

Variations

1. Player cover is on the defensive half of the pitch only.
2. The teams take turns in playing with player cover.
3. The goals are moved farther in on the pitch. Teams score by playing the ball through one of the opposition's goals to a teammate.

Coaching Points

This game enables you to focus on the basic elements of player cover—in particular, whether a defender should break out if a teammate has been outplayed or passed by a direct opponent.

In variation one, the players can move back into their own half of the pitch and organize themselves before player cover is established. This makes the game less physically demanding.

Variation two lowers the intensity for one team, and it may make the game clearer.

In variation three, the players on the team using player cover will become accustomed to moving quickly back down the pitch if they are outplayed or passed.

Keywords

Seek out opponent • Marking • Break out • Sweeper • Retreat

Defensive Transition

Pitch

One half of the pitch, with three zones (1-3) and two large goals, as shown in figure 5.7.

Players

Sixteen: eight versus eight—two defenders, three midfielders, two attackers, and a goalkeeper on each team.

Organization

Two defenders and two attackers from each team are in zones 1 and 3, and the six midfielders are in the center zone.

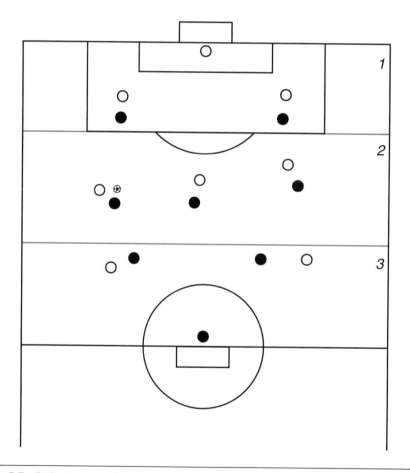

Figure 5.7 Defensive transition.

Description

Normal game; one team at a time uses player cover.

Conditions

Players may not leave their zones.

Scoring

As normal.

Variations

1. The six midfielders may move freely around the pitch.
2. The players in zones 1 and 3 are also allowed in zone 2.
3. All players may move freely around the pitch.
4. Both teams use player cover at the same time.

Coaching Points

This game focuses clearly on the teamwork between the defense, midfield, and attack. The players on the team using player cover will become accustomed to seeking out an opponent quickly when the team loses the ball.

You can introduce variation one once players understand the basic requirements of player cover. This variation requires overview and thus increases the need for players to orient themselves and to be ready to intervene if a teammate is outplayed.

Variation two increases the need for orientation and teamwork between the defenders and the midfielders, and this increases still further in variation three.

In variation four, the game becomes more physically demanding, and you should call rest periods regularly.

Keywords

Seek out opponent • Marking • Break out • Sweeper • Retreat

Focus on the Defense

Pitch

Approximately three quarters of the pitch, with a centerline and two large goals.

Players

Eighteen: nine versus nine, including one sweeper (3) and a goalkeeper on each team. See figure 5.8.

Description

Normal game; the teams take turns using player cover. The offside rule is in force.

Conditions

Player 3 may not go into the opposition's defensive half.

Scoring

As normal.

Variations

1. Both teams use player cover.
2. After an attack is finished or the ball is lost, the team moves back to its own half of the pitch.
3. Each side adds a midfielder.
4. Player 3 may move freely around the pitch.

Coaching Points

This exercise approaches a true game situation, and players should fulfill their regular roles as much as possible. The number of players and their positions should depend on the system the team is using. The illustration shows a team with four at the back, one of whom is a sweeper, and with at least three midfielders. If the team is playing three at the back, you should practice the game with only two players using player cover at the back, and four in the midfield.

You may decide to put the regular defenders and midfielders on one team that should always employ player cover. The other team can consist of midfield and attacking players, plus a goalkeeper. This enables players to practice teamwork in formations similar to those occurring in a game.

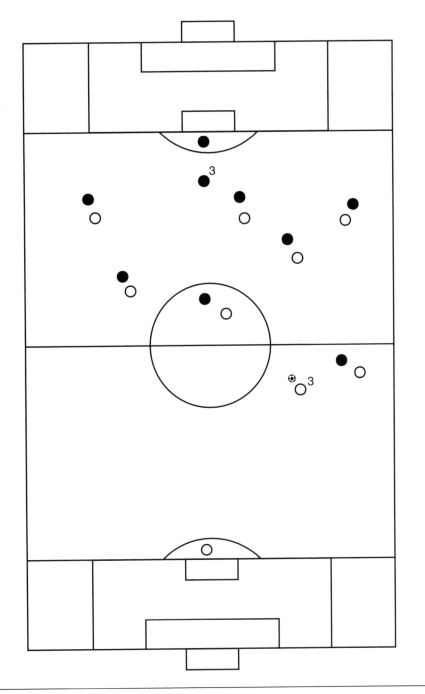

Figure 5.8 Focus on the defense.

Variation one will give players on both teams practice, but the game may become unclear if players concentrate too much on their direct opponents. Players should become accustomed to being aware of both their direct opponents and the rest of the players. The game can also illustrate the difficulties involved when both teams are using player cover and the teams have not selected the same direct opponents.

You can use variation two to clarify situations in the transition from attack to defense, as it should give the players time to establish defensive work. If the opposing team often uses swift counterattacks, these can be controlled; for example, you can stipulate that the team should have three passes in its own half of the field before playing the ball over the centerline.

Variation three approaches a true game situation.

Variation four presents you with an opportunity to focus on how to deal with the problem of being outnumbered. The players should decide whether to break out or whether the sweeper should intervene if the opposition's sweeper moves forward.

Keywords

Seek out opponent • Marking • Break out • Sweeper • Retreat

CHAPTER 6

Zonal Cover

Zonal cover is a way of organizing the defensive game. The thinking behind this form of cover is that you allow players to take responsibility for an area of the pitch, particularly in their own half. This ensures that the team covers the pitch both widthwise and depthwise. The size of an individual player's area depends on the part of the pitch the relevant player is to cover (see figure 6.1).

There are two forms of zonal cover:

- Zonal cover with zonal marking: The players position themselves in a particular area of the pitch and move only in reaction to their teammates.

- Zonal cover with player marking: The players take up positions in a particular area of the pitch and move in accordance with their closest opponent.

A high percentage of elite teams use zonal cover. For example, three of the four semifinalists at the 1998 World Cup in France played with zonal cover (Brazil, France, and Holland), as did just over half of the teams at Euro 96. The strength of zonal cover is that the team's defensive position always forms a compact area consisting of individual player zones. To create a united front, it is important that these areas overlap both lengthwise and widthwise. The movements of the players in figure 6.2 (page 101) illustrate how the united black team protects itself and coordinates the sections (midfield, etc.) and players both horizontally and vertically.

Using the zonal cover principle requires tight organization and a high level of understanding between the players. You should stress the importance of collective understanding in creating a single unit for defensive work.

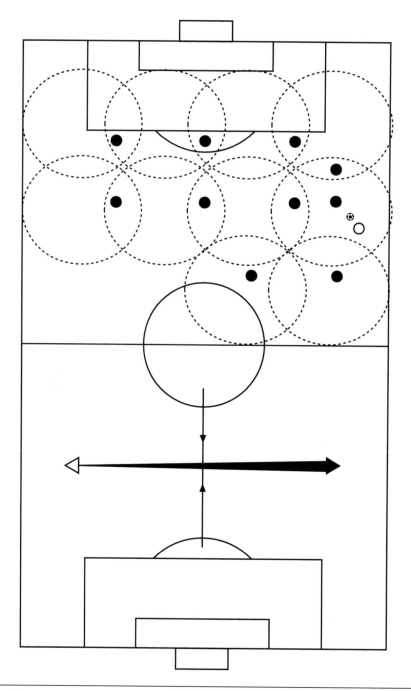

Figure 6.1 Each player is responsible for an area of the pitch.

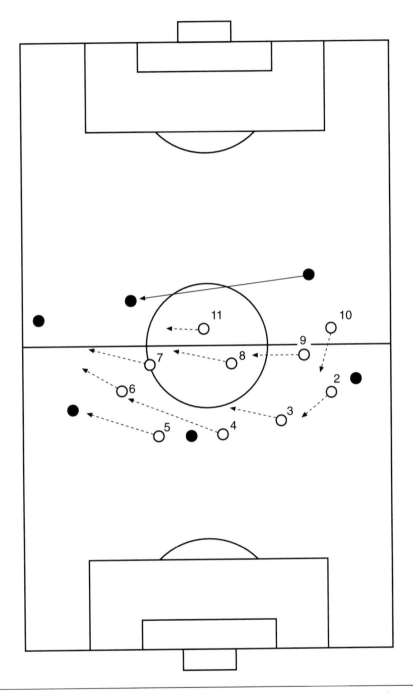

Figure 6.2 Here the black team protects itself by coordinating the sections and players horizontally and vertically.

Zonal Cover With Zonal Marking

Players on a team have their set areas when defending, and they move in accordance with their closest teammate.

It was British teams, particularly Liverpool, who first succeeded in employing an effective form of defense based on zonal cover with zonal marking. Today, many more top European teams, such as Juventus, have developed well-organized zonal cover. The purest example of zonal cover with zonal marking, however, was the Norwegian national side under Egil Olsen. In this team's defensive work, we can almost see strands of elastic between the players, drawing them back and forth in accordance with the game. The synchronized patterns are formed in conjunction with lots of communication between the players.

This form of defensive organization creates an ideal jumping-off point for an attack after winning the ball because there will almost always be good options for playing the ball away from the area where it was won to a well-placed teammate.

Goals

- No free areas are left for the opposition.
- The players can quickly establish an attack when they win the ball.
- The pitch is "made smaller," which makes it more difficult for opponents to keep the ball.

Zonal Marking Fundamentals

A player is responsible for a specific area, and for being in position in relation to the ball and to the closest teammate. If the player with the ball is in this area, the defender should follow the principles of individual defensive action (see chapter 1).

When cover is organized with zonal marking, there should be no free areas near the ball that the opposing team can exploit. While the player in possession on the opposing team is under pressure, the other players on the defensive team should move quickly toward the center of the area around the ball, trying to maintain the distance between themselves and their closest teammates on both sides and up ahead. In this way, the team's defensive organization remains balanced.

When the opposition switches sides in upfield play, the defenders' areas change in turn. Figure 6.2 demonstrates how the white team, by switching sides, maintains the balance of its organization by filling up the new area around the ball.

To play zonal cover with zonal marking, each player must have an overview of the game. The player should know what is happening both close by and around the player with the ball. The defender's movements should be in accord with those of the closest teammate, as shown in figure 6.2. The players should be encouraged to give short instructions such as, "Move left," "Closer," "I'm falling back," and, "Someone's coming across." Communication is vital if players and sections are to reposition quickly.

Zonal Cover With Player Marking

During defensive play, each player is responsible for a particular area of the pitch and marks an opponent in this area until exchanging opponents with a teammate or until the ball is won.

Zonal cover with player marking is a form of defensive organization more frequently used than zonal cover with zonal marking. British teams, in particular, have inspired people to use this type of defensive organization, which gives individual defenders responsibility for marking in their own areas. There are many examples of how a player becomes a specialist in marking within a set area. The Dane Jan Heintze and Arsenal player Tony Adams have often demonstrated the positioning ability that makes them important links in their teams' defensive chains while leaving them in a position to win the ball from their opponents.

Goals

- Closely covering an opponent near the ball in the last third of the pitch.
- No free opponents in the defensive area.
- Quickly establish an attack when the ball is regained.

Player Marking Fundamentals

A player is responsible for a specific area and should mark any opponents in it. Player marking follows the principles of individual defensive action (see chapter 1). The defender should judge position within the area relative to the opponent, the center of the game, and any teammates in the vicinity. The player should also have an overview of the positions of teammates, which will make it possible to advise them regarding their positions if, say, an opponent moves behind them. In order to obtain this overview, the player should use split vision: besides registering the

German defender Matthias Sammer was highly skilled in making contact with the opponent in his area and following him until another team member took over.

opponent and the game, the player should also be aware of what is happening inside the area of responsibility.

During zonal cover with player marking, players must coordinate their exchanges of opponents. We will deal with this issue later in the chapter.

Practices and Drills

You can use the following exercises to coach zonal cover with both zonal and player marking. You should emphasize the format you want the team to practice. The first two drills (Defensive Shift and Staying Connected) can be used for warm-up.

Defensive Shift

Pitch

Quartered area on the sideline approximately 16×16 meters.

Players

Nine: four attackers (white) and four defenders (black); one is the "playing station."

Description

The attackers should be outside the squares and must take two touches. The "playing station" player is inside the square area and should play the ball out into a new area. The four defenders each begin in a separate square. When the ball is in area A, the two defenders who are nearest should move outside their squares, while the two remaining defenders move into the vacated squares. If the ball is played to area B, the two near defenders should move out of the squares, while the remaining two move into the adjacent squares, and so on. By playing the ball into the square, the attackers can vary the changes in area to a greater extent. Attackers and defenders rotate positions every three minutes. See figure 6.3.

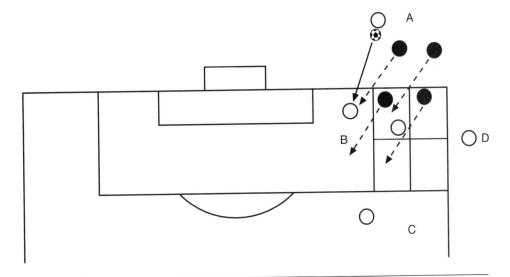

Figure 6.3 Defensive shift.

Staying Connected

Pitch

The center circle and the surrounding area.

Players

Ten: six attackers (white) and four defenders (black).

Description

The six attackers are divided on either side of the centerline with two outside the circle and one inside it, as shown in figure 6.4. The defenders may not win the ball. The attacking players must take two touches. When the ball is played over the centerline and outside the circle, the two defenders from that side of the pitch should move into their own semicircle, and the other defenders should move out of the circle. If the ball is played into the center circle, the two far defenders should move into the circle area. That is to say, when the ball is on one half of the pitch, the two appropriate defenders should be outside the circle, while the two far defenders should either move into their own semicircle or across into the far semicircle if the ball is played into this area. Attackers and defenders rotate positions every three minutes.

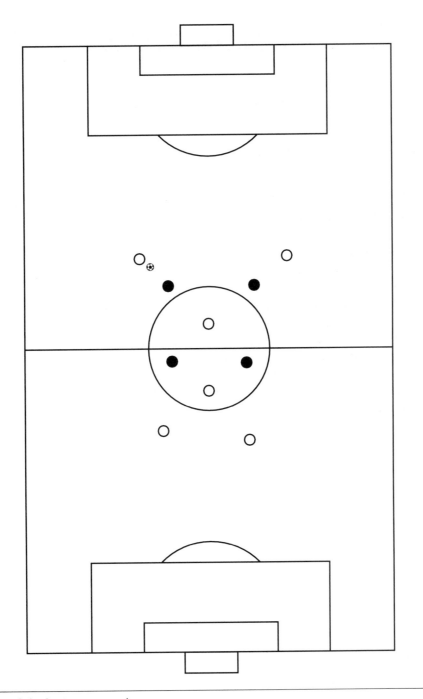

Figure 6.4 Staying connected.

Midfield Defense

Pitch

One half of the pitch, consisting of two zones (1 and 2) and four small goals parallel to the centerline between zones 1 and 2, as shown in figure 6.5.

Players

Ten: five versus five.

Organization

The black team plays from the baseline toward the goals in zone 1, while the white team plays from the centerline toward the goals in zone 2.

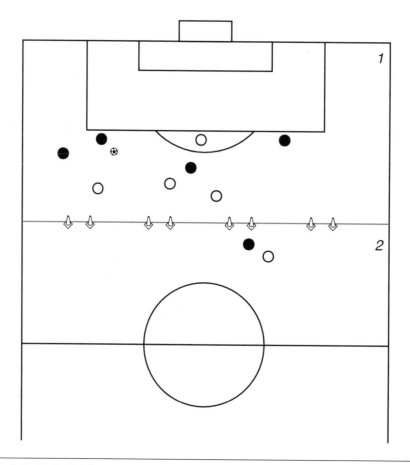

Figure 6.5   Midfield defense.

Description

Normal game.

Conditions

The black team may only score from zone 1 and the white team only from zone 2. When white wins the ball after scoring, the team plays it into zone 2, and vice versa for black if that team wins the ball in zone 2. The first pass after the ball has been won is free, so no opponent may touch the ball until a player other than the passer has played it.

Scoring

Goals are scored in the small goals.

Variations

1. When a team scores, it remains in possession of the ball.
2. One more player is added to each team.

Coaching Points

This exercise primarily trains the horizontal movements of a team section (midfield, etc.) in defensive play (i.e., sideways movements). The defenders should concentrate on moving their areas relative to the area around the ball.

In variation one, the defending team has to reorganize quickly into zonal cover again. It is vital, therefore, for players to communicate and coordinate the formation.

Variation two allows the defending team to work together more easily in directing the opposition's game and increasing the concentration of players around the ball.

Keywords for Zonal Marking

Horizontal balance • Overview • Communication

Keywords for Man-to-Man Marking

Timing • Guide • Overview • Split vision

Defensive Pressure

Pitch

Approximately one third of the pitch, with five small goals about 10 meters from the centerline and two large goals on the goal line. See figure 6.6.

Players

Eleven: six versus five; the white team has five players and the black team has six, two of whom are goalkeepers.

Organization

The white team defends the small goals.

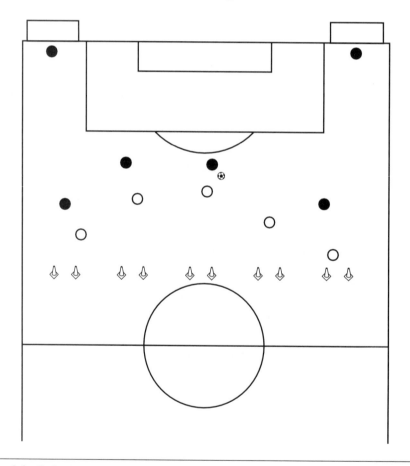

Figure 6.6 Defensive pressure.

Description

Normal game; the two goalkeepers on the black team can be brought into the game as backs.

Conditions

The white team is allowed no more than three touches.

Scoring

The black team scores in the small goals, and the white team scores in the large goals.

Variations

1. The black team can score double by dribbling through the goals.
2. Another player is added to the black team.

Coaching Points

The white team outnumbers the black team out on the pitch, and so can employ compact zonal cover and pressure the player with the ball a long way up the pitch. You can highlight how the team as a whole can break forward relative to the location of the ball. When the goalkeeper puts the ball back into play, the white team may have problems getting organized quickly enough. It is therefore important for white team players to try to harry the upfield play of the black team until the defensive formation is in position.

Variation one encourages the black team to challenge the white defenders; the white team players, therefore, need to think about backward and sideways movement.

Variation two increases the pressure on the white team to organize its defensive formation quickly.

Keywords for Zonal Marking

Horizontal balance • Overview • Communication

Keywords for Man-to-Man Marking

Judge • Guide • Overview • Split vision

Possession Defense

Pitch

One half of the pitch, divided into two zones (1 and 2) with small goals (four meters wide) positioned parallel with the centerline between zones 1 and 2, as shown in figure 6.7.

Players

Ten: five versus four and one goalkeeper.

Organization

The white team has four players (plus a goalkeeper) and the black team has five.

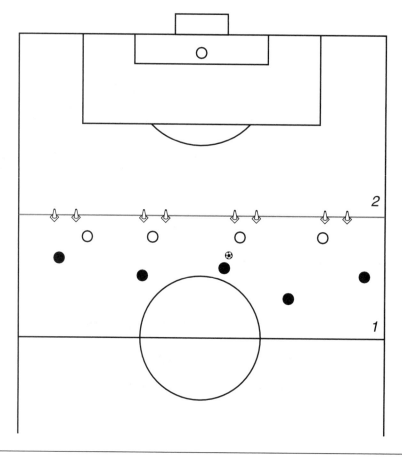

Figure 6.7 Possession defense.

Description

Normal game; the white team defends the large goal and the black team starts with the ball in zone 1.

Conditions

The black team may only enter zone 2 by playing through one of the small goals. If the white team wins the ball, the players should try to hold onto it.

Scoring

The black team scores in the large goal. The white team (including the goalkeeper) scores one goal by maintaining possession of the ball for a minimum of six passes.

Variations

1. Two wide (20 meter) goals are on the centerline instead of four.
2. One more player is added to each team.

Coaching Points

This exercise is primarily aimed at training the white team's horizontal movement in defensive play (sideways movement). The defenders should concentrate on moving their positional areas relative to the ball.

In variation one, the defending team has to reorganize swiftly into a new zonal formation and must communicate and coordinate to this end. Likewise, the need to quickly cover the player with the ball increases.

In variation two, the defending team will find it easier to work together to direct the opposition's game and increase the concentration of players around the ball.

Keywords for Zonal Marking

Horizontal balance • Overview • Communication

Keywords for Man-to-Man Marking

Judge • Guide • Overview • Split vision

Marking the Attack

Pitch

Approximately one third of the pitch, divided into three zones (1-3) with two large goals.

Players

Ten: five versus five, including two goalkeepers.

Organization

White 2 and 3 and black 4 and 5 start in zone 1, while white 6 and 7 and black 8 and 9 start in zone 3, as shown in figure 6.8.

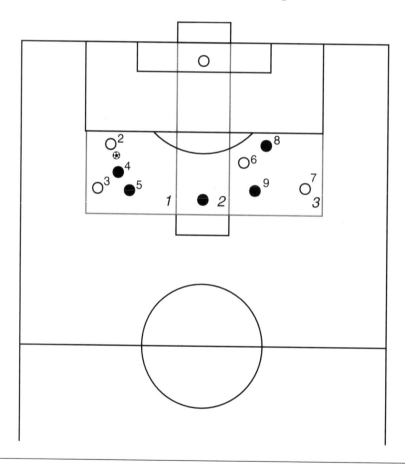

Figure 6.8   Marking the attack.

Description

Normal game.

Conditions

Players 2, 3, 4, and 5 may go into zones 1 and 2. The team in possession may not play the ball forward in zones 2 and 3. Players 6, 7, 8, and 9 may go into zones 2 and 3.

Scoring

As normal.

Variations

1. The team in possession may play the ball forward in zone 2.
2. One more player is added to each team.

Coaching Points

This game focuses on the horizontal and vertical movement patterns of the covering team. Zone 2 defines the overlapping horizontal areas, so the defenders have a direction of play in which to extend their sideways movement. At the same time, they can gain experience of the offensive options zonal cover offers when play is switched.

Variation one increases the need for the defending team to coordinate defensive movements efficiently.

Variation two introduces more players to the defensive situation, increasing the need for overview and communication.

Keywords for Zonal Marking

Horizontal balance • Overview • Communication

Keywords for Man-to-Man Marking

Judge • Guide • Overview • Split vision

Defensive Adjusting

Pitch

One half of the pitch, divided into three zones (1-3), as shown in figure 6.9.

Players

Eighteen: nine versus nine, with one goalkeeper on each team. Two players on each team are counter-running players (10 and 11).

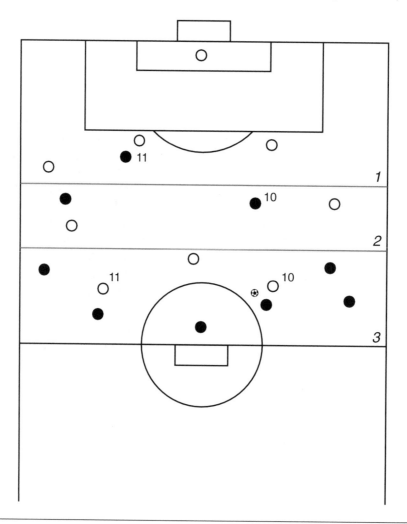

Figure 6.9   Defensive adjusting.

Description

Normal game, including the offside rule; the ball can only be played into the attacking zone if either 10 or 11 has touched it in the center zone (2).

Conditions

Players 10 and 11 should be in the attacking zone when the opposition has the ball. Only 10 and 11 may touch the ball in the center zone, and they have a maximum of three touches on contact with the ball.

Scoring

As normal.

Variation

Players 10 and 11 do not have to have touched the ball before it is played into the attacking zone.

Coaching Points

Because of 10 and 11's counter-runs, the opposition's attackers will have to change position many times, thereby forcing constant adjustment of the defending team's zonal cover. If the team performing zonal cover is using player marking, the defenders at the back must decide how far to follow 10 and 11, while the other players must decide who should take over marking 10 and 11 when they come down the pitch. The different sections should communicate effectively when the attackers move into new positions. This exercise requires a balance between the relative positions of all players in the same vertical lines on the pitch, from the front of the attack to the rear of the defense.

In the variation, the attacking team has greater freedom of movement, and the defending team's use of overview and communication increases.

Keywords for Zonal Marking

Horizontal balance • Overview • Communication

Keywords for Man-to-Man Marking

Judge • Guide • Overview • Split vision

Midfield Cover

Pitch

One half of the pitch, with 10 cones positioned on the goal line and centerline.

Players

Fourteen: seven versus seven.

Organization

Both teams are organized into two-section formations (4-3 formations). See figure 6.10.

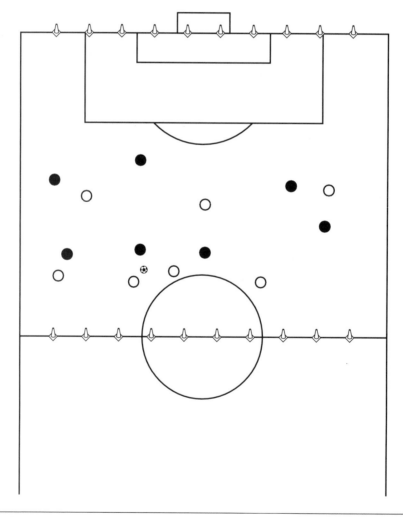

Figure 6.10 Midfield cover.

Description

Normal game, including the offside rule; each team defends and attacks the 10 cones.

Conditions

The players have no more than two touches on contact with the ball.

Scoring

A point is scored when one of the opposition's cones is hit.

Variations

1. A point is scored when the ball is played between two cones.
2. No restrictions are placed on touches.

Coaching Points

The pitch is wide, requiring the defenders to cover large areas. This calls for both full concentration and physical energy to create a compact covering unit.

Variation one increases the need for tight cover of the player with the ball.

The need for cover and support is increased again in variation two, when the attackers can move freely, allowing them, for instance, to dribble.

Keywords for Zonal Marking

Horizontal balance • Overview • Communication

Keywords for Man-to-Man Marking

Judge • Guide • Overview • Split vision

Organize the "D"

Pitch

Approximately two thirds of the pitch and two large goals.

Players

Eighteen: nine versus nine, including a goalkeeper on each team.

Organization

Both teams are organized into two four-player sections. The regular centerline divides the two sections of the pitch so that the goal range for each team will be somewhat different. See figure 6.11.

Description

Normal game, including the offside rule (ignoring the centerline).

Conditions

On their own half of the pitch, the players may have no more than two touches, and the team may only have five passes before playing the ball over the centerline. The team may not play the ball back into its own half of the pitch.

Scoring

As normal.

Variations

1. Both teams must always have two players over the centerline.
2. The team defending the large "half" must play the ball over the center after a maximum of two passes. The goalkeeper may also play the ball directly up into the opposition's half of the pitch.

Coaching Points

This game trains the defensive section's ability to organize quickly. Since the opposing team should play the ball quickly across into the defending team's half, the front section must attempt to direct the opposition's upfield play to help the rear section of defenders, so that players are concentrated in the appropriate area of the opposition's half. The team defending the small "half" will find it easier to create a compact unit than the team with the large "half."

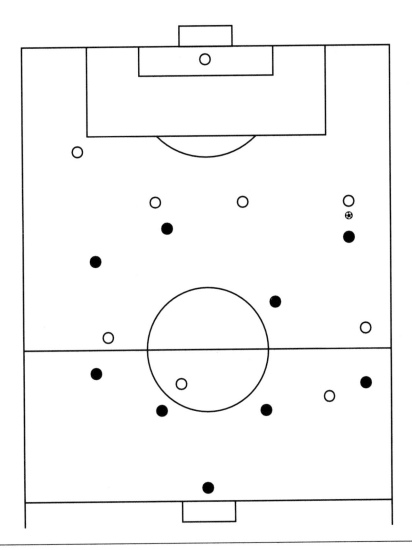

Figure 6.11 Organize the "D."

In variation one, the rear defenders should constantly be aware of the positions of the two opponents and should bear this in mind when attacking. One of the defenders at the back must direct teammates. This applies both when the players from the defensive section are breaking forward into attack and when they are retreating. The defending team will also gain experience in switching to attacking play.

In variation two, the defending team should be prepared for the long ball. The players in the front section should take up positions to try and force the pass out to the wing. The players at the back should move horizontally in the direction of the pass and should communicate and judge whether they should try to intercept the delivery or simply wait.

Keywords for Zonal Marking

Horizontal balance • Overview • Communication

Keywords for Man-to-Man Marking

Judge • Guide • Overview • Split vision

Taking Over Marking

A defender takes over marking an opponent from a teammate when the opponent enters the defender's area and is farther from the teammate's area than the player the defender is currently marking. That is, two defenders (white team) take over one another's marking responsibilities when their direct opponents (black team) switch between their areas (figure 6.12).

This principle is used by teams who, either wholly or partially, use zonal cover with player marking (see page 103).

Goals

- To avoid leaving players unmarked.
- To limit the running work of individual defenders.

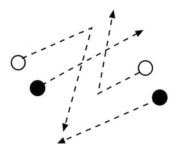

Figure 6.12 When two attackers (black) switch areas, their two defenders (white) take over each other's marking.

Fundamentals

The following main points are applicable to the players and to you as coach with regard to the principle of taking over marking.

Speed

When taking over an opponent, the defender should move quickly toward the new player and take up an appropriate defensive position.

Judgment

The two defenders marking the attackers who are changing zones should judge whether switching opponents might be too dangerous. If the attackers are a long way apart, it may be preferable to delay the switch until a more appropriate moment. Figure 6.13 shows the problems that can result from markers switching opponents. If players 2 and 4 decide to exchange their direct opponents, 10 and 11 will be free for a short time. Player 10, if free, would be particularly dangerous in this situation because there is no other opponent between 10 and the goal. Player 2 could remedy this by leaving 11 early and moving backward as soon as it is clear that 11 wants to run in—but then 11 will become free if 10 does not move out onto the wing.

When it is not possible to take over attackers in this way, the defenders should follow their opponents—even if this takes them outside their areas—until the situation has been resolved or until a teammate can take over the opponent. The disadvantage of this is that the defenders (players 2 and 4 in figure 6.13) become displaced and end up outside their areas.

During practice, players must get some idea of when they should switch opponents with other team members, and when they should follow the attacker out of their area.

Communication

Communication is a key concept in switching opponents correctly. The players should become accustomed to constantly keeping each other informed of both their own and their opponents' positions during defensive work. When opponents are about to move between two areas, the defenders involved must communicate briefly, calling, for example, "I'll go with him," "I'll take him," or, "Someone's coming."

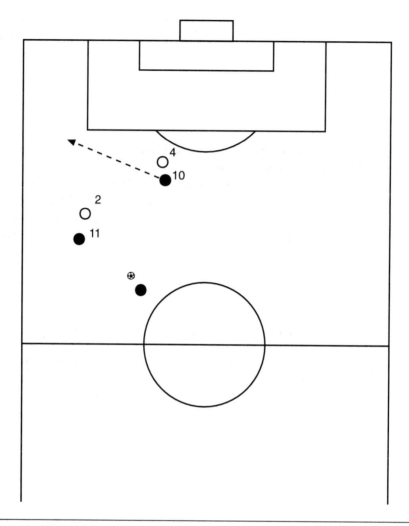

Figure 6.13 If 2 and 4 decide to switch marking, 10 and 11 will be free for a short time, leaving 10 with a good opportunity for a goal.

Practices and Drills

Following is a range of exercises for practicing taking over players using zonal cover. The first three drills can be used as warm-up exercises: Cover the Takeover, Zonal Cover Warm-Up, and Unbalanced Cover.

Cover the Takeover

Players

Six.

Description

Player 1 dribbles toward 2, who runs toward 1. At about the halfway point, 2 takes over the ball and continues the run. Player 3 follows (marks) 1, and 4 marks 2 until 2 takes over the ball from 1, after which 3 follows 2 and 4 marks 1. Player 5 takes over the ball from 2 and dribbles toward 6, who runs forward toward 5. Player 3 now marks 5 and 4 marks 6, until 6 takes over the ball from 5, after which 3 follows 6, and so on. See figure 6.14.

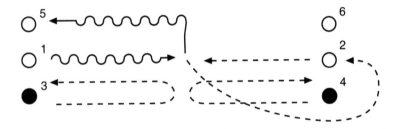

Figure 6.14   Cover the takeover.

Zonal Cover Warm-Up

Pitch

Approximately 16.5 × 20 meters, divided into four zones with two cones placed in each zone, as shown in figure 6.15.

Players

Eight: four versus four.

Conditions

Each team has one player in each zone and defends four cones. Only the team with the ball may change zones (an overlap of one meter is acceptable).

Description

Normal game; teams score points by hitting the opposition's cones.

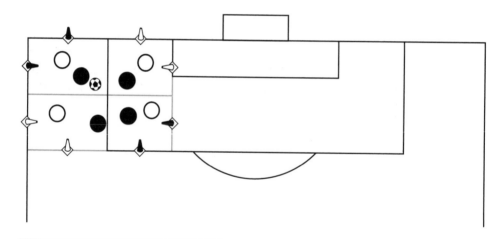

Figure 6.15 Zonal cover warm-up.

Unbalanced Cover

Pitch

An elongated penalty area divided into three zones (1-3) in which the center zone (2) is divided into three subzones, as shown in figure 6.16.

Players

Eight: three versus three and two "jokers" who are always on the side of the team with the ball.

Conditions

Both teams should have one player in each of the three subzones. Only the team with the ball may change zones (an overlap of one meter is acceptable). The jokers should be in zones 1 and 3. They may only touch the ball twice. The ball should not stop moving in zones 1 and 3.

Description

The jokers should play the ball back to the team they received it from. A point is scored if the same player touches the ball in all three subzones and if both jokers touch the ball without the team losing possession—that is, as long as two players from the opposing team have not touched the ball in succession.

Variation

The defending team can also change zones.

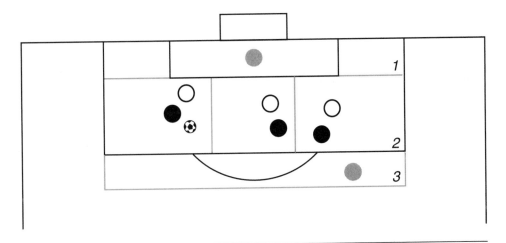

Figure 6.16   Unbalanced cover.

Defensive Cooperation

Pitch

Approximately one quarter of the pitch, consisting of two zones (1 and 2) and a large goal.

Players

Eight: two midfielders (6 and 8) and two attackers (10 and 11) versus one midfielder (7), two defenders (3 and 5), and a goalkeeper (1).

Organization

The midfield players (6, 7, and 8) are in zone 2, while the rest of the players are in zone 1. Player 6 starts with the ball. See figure 6.17.

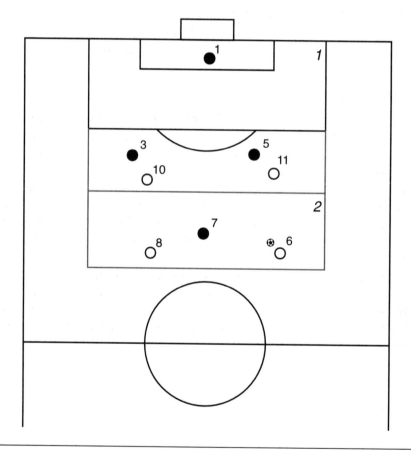

Figure 6.17 Defensive cooperation.

Description

Player 6 or 8 should pass to 10 or 11 when appropriate.

Conditions

The players may not change zones. A one-meter offside rule specifies that attackers must be more than one meter offside to be penalized. Players 6 and 8 cannot score.

Scoring

The attacking team scores in the large goal. The defending team scores a point when the ball is played in the air from 3 or 5 to 7.

Variations

1. Zone 1 is extended.
2. The players from zone 1 may also go into zone 2.
3. One extra midfield player is added to each team, and the players from zone 2 (apart from one on the attacking team) may go into zone 1.

Coaching Points

This game focuses on defensive cooperation between 3 and 5, who should mark 10 and 11 closely. When 10 and 11 change places (which they should be encouraged to do), 3 and 5 have to switch opponents. If either 10 or 11 runs into an offside position, the defenders should allow them to run. The practice enables you to highlight the importance of a quick changeover and of communication between 3 and 5.

Variations one and two increase the need for communication since the distance between 10 and 11 may be greater when they start the switch.

Variation three focuses not only on the coordination between 3 and 5, but also on how they coordinate with the two midfielders. If one of the opposition's midfielders breaks forward and an attacker moves farther back down the pitch, the defenders should switch opponents with the appropriate midfielder.

Keywords

Speed • Judgment • Communication

Defensive Coordination

Pitch

One half of the pitch, consisting of two zones (1 and 2) with a large goal.

Players

Sixteen: eight versus eight, of which the defending team has three marking players (2, 3, and 5), a sweeper (4), and a goalkeeper (1).

Organization

In zone 2, the attacking team (white) has four players and the defending team (black) has three. The remaining players are in zone 1. See figure 6.18.

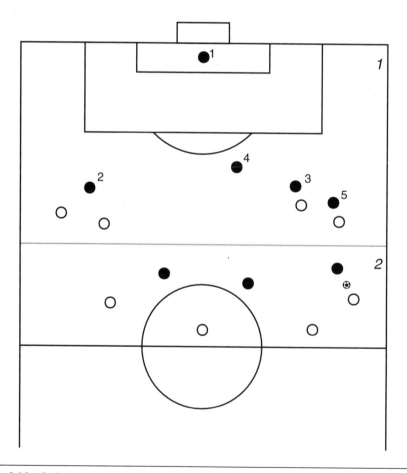

Figure 6.18 Defensive coordination.

Description

Normal game.

Conditions

Players may not leave their zones. The offside rule is in force.

Scoring

The attacking team scores in the large goal. The defending team scores points by dribbling the ball over the centerline.

Variations

1. The players from zone 1 may also go into zone 2.
2. All players may move freely over the pitch.

Coaching Points

This game highlights how 2, 3, and 5 coordinate defensively, both between themselves and in conjunction with the sweeper (4). The attackers should be encouraged to change places frequently, giving the defenders practice in switching their opponents.

In variation one, the defensive work is made more difficult for the marking players, challenging their ability to judge when a changeover of opponents should take place. You should halt the game if the players neglect a changeover opportunity or if they switch opponents at an inappropriate moment.

Variation two is closer to an actual game situation and enables you to concentrate on the communication between defense and midfield. If one of the outer markers moves in toward the center, for example, the midfield player on that side should fall back and cover the free area.

Keywords

Speed • Judgment • Communication

Cover the Zone

Pitch

Approximately one quarter of the pitch, with three zones (1-3) and six cones placed on each team's goal line, as shown in figure 6.19.

Players

Twelve: six versus six.

Organization

Each team has two players in each zone.

Description

Normal game.

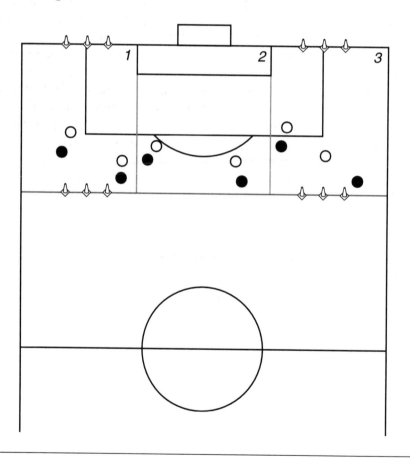

Figure 6.19 Cover the zone.

Conditions

Players on the defending team may not switch zones. Players on the team with the ball may switch zones with another team member. (Players who are in the process of switching zones may be in the same zone within two meters of the border between the zones.)

Scoring

Teams score points by hitting one of the opposition's cones.

Variations

1. A one-player, one-meter offside rule is applied.
2. Each team should have at least one player in each zone.

Coaching Points

You should explain that the players in the zones have to play according to the principle of zonal cover with player marking. During the game, defenders will be "forced" to take over opponents and will therefore become used to keeping an eye on opponents in the adjacent zone(s). The defenders should learn something of the difficulties of taking over an opponent who is some distance away.

When you combine this with variation one, in which the defending team will move forward more, the defenders will appreciate the advantages of maintaining a closely knit team during a changeover.

In variation two, defenders should start in their original zones. When their opponents change places, the players have to decide whether to switch opponents or continue as they are.

Keywords

Speed • Judgment • Communication

Zone to Zone

Pitch

Approximately one quarter of the pitch, with three zones (1-3)—in which zones 1 and 3 are divided into two areas—and two large goals. See figure 6.20.

Players

Fourteen: six versus six, plus a goalkeeper on each team.

Organization

Each team has three players in zones 1 and 3, plus a goalkeeper in either zone 1 or zone 3.

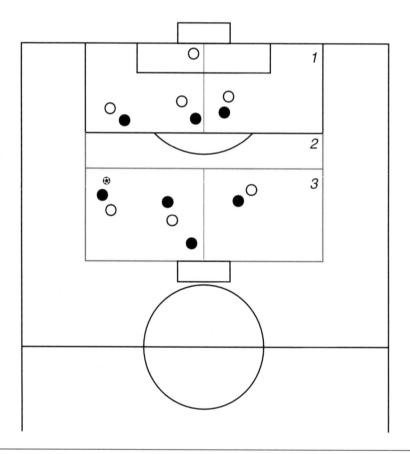

Figure 6.20 Zone to zone.

Description

Normal game.

Conditions

Players must remain in their zones. The defending team should assign one player to each of the small zones; that is, only one defender may move freely within zone 1 and another within zone 3. The team with the ball must always have one player in each of the small zones.

Scoring

As normal in the two large goals.

Variations

1. Players are no longer restricted to the small zones. Each team should, however, have at least one player in each zone.
2. The team in possession does not need to have one player in each of the small zones.
3. When a goal is scored, the direction of attack reverses, so defenders become attackers.

Coaching Points

This game focuses on coordination between the defender who is not bound to one zone and the other two defenders. If there are two attackers in one of the small zones, the defender who is bound to that zone should always be aware of the positions of teammates and opponents. This player should decide whether and when it is appropriate to switch opponents with a teammate. Players should, as a rule, mark the opponent closest to the boundary of the zone.

Variation one gives the defenders more freedom but also demands cooperation and, to be certain, communication between the players. Variation one will come naturally once the players become used to the game.

In variation two, the defending team will at times be outnumbered in one of the small zones. This gives you an opportunity to focus on what should be covered when players are unmarked.

You can use variation three to highlight the transition from attack to defense. The variation can also be used to rotate the game so certain players are not always defending.

Keywords

Speed • Judgment • Communication

CHAPTER 7

Combination Defense

In combination defense, a team organizes its defensive play in such a way that some players use player cover and others use zonal cover.

The idea of combining player and zonal cover is to use the advantages of both, while at the same time eliminating their disadvantages. Teams playing 3-5-2 often use combination defense. Player cover in defense is the most important aspect of this type of defensive organization. Players feel most comfortable when the opposition's strikers are constantly covered by the two defenders, called marking players, because their responsibilities are clear. This can allow other players to be more flexible with their defensive roles. Sometimes teams using combination defense have their midfielders use player cover on the opposition's playmaker. The idea behind this is to minimize the space available to the playmaker—and with it, this player's value to the opposing team. A midfield with five players can still cover the pitch's width and depth, even if one of their number is performing player cover.

The greatest disadvantage of combination defense is that it can easily lead to confusion and an inappropriate distribution of players, such as when a marking player is pushed into the zone of a team member who is performing zonal cover.

The successful Danish national team of the 1980s and the early 1990s usually played in a 3-5-2 formation with combination defense. Two central defenders used player cover with player marking, while the rest of the players had their own zones. At the 1998 World Cup in France, Cannavaro used player cover on Tore André Flo in the Italy-Norway game. At the same time, the Italians were playing with Bergomi as a sweeper, while the other players used zonal marking.

137

Goals

- Ensure that important opponents are tightly covered.
- Make better use of players' defensive skills.

Combination Defense Fundamentals

To create an effective combination defense, players with the various defensive tasks need a clear understanding of the overall purpose. During training, you should be aware of situations that may lead to misunderstandings regarding defense. This applies particularly to situations in which the defensive tasks overlap, such as when a player covering a particular opponent follows that opponent into an area where a teammate's coverage is zonal. While this creates a two-versus-one situation in that zone, it also opens up a free area that other players must close. The other players should readjust their areas in response to the game situation. Players must have an overview of the defensive tasks and positions of the surrounding players in order to avoid misunderstandings, and they must also communicate any moves they are making.

Point cover is a special form of combination defense in which one of the opposition's players is covered closely during all or part of a game. Regardless of the form of cover the team as a whole uses, point cover means that a player should concentrate solely on using man-to-man cover against the relevant player. If the opposing team has a player who is an important factor in its attacking play (e.g., a good playmaker), you may decide to have that attacker point covered. The defender carrying out point cover deviates from the regular cover principles in that this player should not react to the game situation by varying the distance from the opponent. The defender must concentrate on maintaining this task. Point cover should prevent the opponent from being played, and passing options should be limited when the attacker does receive the ball.

Practices and Drills

When practicing combination defense, you can use the exercises under zonal and player cover (in chapters 5 and 6) as well as the ones listed here (starting on page 140).

The close battle between the Italian Cannavaro and the Norwegian Tore André Flo was a game within a game at the World Cup. The powerful Cannavaro used his speed to beat Flo to the ball.

Coordinating the Combination Defense

Pitch

Approximately one half of the pitch, divided into two zones (1 and 2) where zone 1 is inside zone 2.

Players

Twelve: seven versus five. The white team is three defenders (2, 3, and 4), three midfielders (6, 7, and 8), and a goalkeeper. The black team is two strikers (10 and 11) and three midfielders (5, 6, and 9).

Organization

Normal game; the midfield players are restricted to zone 1 and the rest of the players can move freely about the pitch. See figure 7.1.

Description

The goalkeeper starts the game by playing the ball to a black-team midfielder.

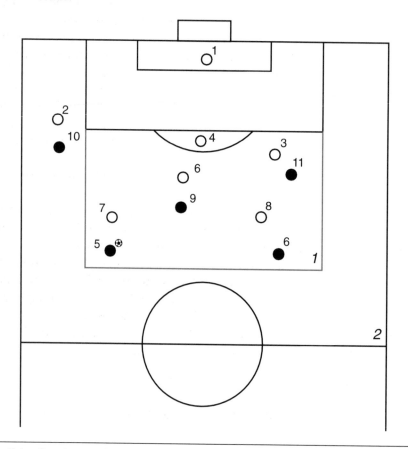

Figure 7.1   Coordinating the combination defense.

Conditions

White 2 and 3 should use player cover on 10 and 11, while white 6 uses player cover on black 9. The other white-team players use zonal cover.

Scoring

The black team scores as normal. The white team scores by completing five passes without interruption and then playing the ball back to the goalkeeper.

Variations

1. Players 9 and 6 may move beyond zone 1.
2. The black team gets an extra player (8) who may not score.
3. The black-team midfielders have a maximum of three touches.
4. The zonal restrictions are removed.

Coaching Points

This exercise highlights the teamwork necessary between players with different forms of covering tasks. In the defensive game, player 4 should constantly register the positions of the two players employing player cover (2 and 3). Player 4 should assess his or her own position relative to the ball and to 2 and 3, and then judge whether to break forward on the midfield as backup if the midfield players look like they are being outnumbered. In the white midfield, 7 and 8 should concentrate on their own areas while bearing in mind the possibility of breaking out if black 9 breaks free of 6 and 4 is not in a position to intervene.

Variation one increases the need for the white-team players to take in the entire situation.

With variation two, the black team can vary the game with another option, forcing the white team to reorganize more quickly and thereby increasing the opportunities for misunderstandings.

In variation three, a white-team defender can put extra pressure on the player with the ball after two touches, which also enables teammates to get into better covering positions for winning the ball.

Variation four extends the playing arena, which increases the demands on the observation skills of the defenders regarding their relative positions and coordinated moves.

Keywords

Clarity • Understanding • Overview • Communication

Communicating With Combination Coverage

Pitch

One half of the pitch with one large goal, and three small goals on the centerline, as shown in figure 7.2.

Players

Fourteen: eight versus six. The white team consists of four defenders (2, 3, 4, and 5), three midfielders (6, 7, and 8), and a goalkeeper (1). The black team consists of two strikers (10 and 11) and four midfielders (6, 7, 8, and 9).

Description

Normal game.

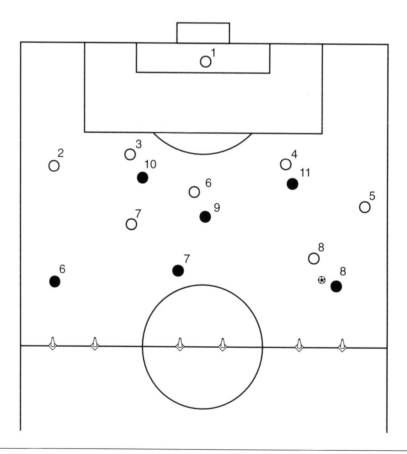

Figure 7.2   Communicating with combination coverage.

Conditions

White 3 and 4 should use player cover on 10 and 11, while 6 marks black 9. The other white players use zonal cover.

Scoring

The black team scores as normal. The white team scores in the three small goals on the centerline.

Variations

1. The black team has a maximum of three touches.
2. A sweeper is added to the white team and a midfielder to the black team.
3. Both teams have one more player in midfield and the pitch is extended to about three quarters of the full pitch.

Coaching Points

The game is based on a defensive/midfield formation (white team) playing against an attacking/midfield formation (black team). The white team should ensure that its teamwork is well coordinated. The back row players should focus on how they can prevent free space from opening up in the finishing zone or when the strikers (10 and 11) move across. Depending on the individual game situation, the backs using zonal cover may move into positions in the free areas. Likewise, players should be aware of how they can establish "elastic" zonal cover along the sidelines through teamwork between the backs and the forward midfielders.

Besides maintaining contact with the rear defenders, 7 and 8 in the white team's midfield should concentrate on their own areas while bearing in mind the possibility of breaking out should black 9 elude 6.

With variation one, a white-team defender can put more pressure on the player with the ball after two touches, while teammates can take up better covering positions for winning the ball.

Variation two teaches players to coordinate with a sweeper, with particular emphasis on the sweeper's position ahead of the team-mate who is using player cover.

Variation three extends the playing area and thus increases the need for players to understand each other and adapt constantly to cover situations, particularly in midfield.

Keywords

Clarity • Understanding • Overview • Communication

Marking the Striker

Pitch

One half of the pitch with two large goals.

Players

Sixteen: seven versus seven, plus a goalkeeper on each team.

Organization

The white team plays in a 3-4 formation. See figure 7.3.

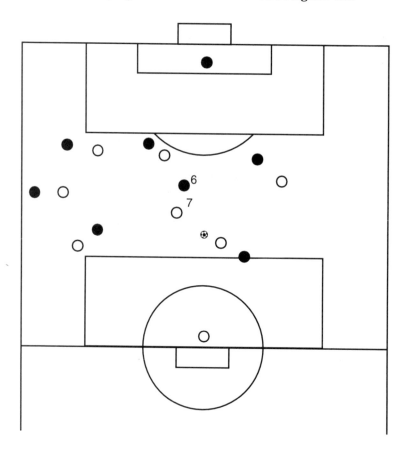

Figure 7.3   Marking the striker.

Description

Normal game.

Conditions

Both the black and white teams play with zonal cover, and one player on the black team (6) plays point cover against a white-team player (7).

Scoring

As normal, but goals count double if 7 scores or is the penultimate person to touch the ball before the goal.

Variation

During the game, another player on the black team may point cover instead of 6.

Coaching Points

This game focuses on how the black team should organize its defense when playing with point cover.

Players should attend to their defensive tasks while keeping one eye on 6's position and being ready to provide support. Player 6 may often get into situations where it appears that intervention could help a teammate but must not stop point covering the opponent.

The variation splits up the task of point cover. In order to make better use of the offensive options of a player who is point covering, you can divide the task so that the closer of the two players leaves point cover when the opposition wins the ball. It is important that the two players coordinate closely in this task.

Keywords

Clarity • Understanding • Overview • Communication

The Croatian Prosinecki has dazzling technique and has not only filled the role of playmaker for his country, but also for the Real Madrid, among others. Kim Vilfort's task for most of this 1997 World Cup qualifier, therefore, was to point cover him.

CHAPTER 8

Team Defensive Depth

One of the most effective attacking weapons is the ball played behind the defense. For this reason, coaches are always keen to work out ways of preventing the appearance of free areas behind the back row. The simplest solution is to play with a sweeper. This enables the team to guarantee depth in the back row. Players in this position usually have amazing insight into how game situations develop. Some teams play both with a sweeper in the back row and a "libero" in the midfield; others play with one sweeper who is often positioned ahead of the back row, thus moving the defense forward on the pitch. Italy, for instance, played Franco Baresi as sweeper in midfield for parts of games for many years.

Some teams have no sweeper and use a flat back four. This method can be successful in certain situations. In the majority of situations, a player in the back row, deciding that a situation may become dangerous, creates depth by moving farther down the pitch than teammates closer to the ball.

Depth in the defensive game is also about unity between defense, midfield, and attack. Teams often have too great a distance between two of these sections, enabling the opposition to play past one section without the next one being able to cover the pass or establish a backup.

There were many instances during the 1998 World Cup where teams exploited the disadvantages of a flat back four, and a substantial number of goals were scored from passes over the back row on to a forward-running player. The first example came in the opening game, in which the Brazilian midfielder Dunga played a hard ball from around the center circle across the Scottish back row to a forward-breaking right back, Cafu, on the edge of the Scottish penalty area. Cafu elegantly brought the ball down and scored. Spain used this same maneuver to score its second goal against

Nigeria. This time, it was Hierro in midfield who put a long ball past the defense to a forward-breaking Raul, who speedily put the ball in the back of the net.

Goals

- To prevent an opponent from continuing unhindered up the pitch with the ball.
- To support a teammate attempting to win the ball.
- To capture the opposition's deep passes.

Defensive Depth Fundamentals

Depth in defensive play is created by one or more players not pressuring the player with the ball, who move closer to their own goal than to the ball and take up positions on the diagonal line between the ball and the goal.

This ensures that the team always has one or more defenders behind the back row or the area around the ball. The defense will be in a position to win a pass from the opposition into this depth and reinforce the team member who is pressuring the player with the ball. Every player on a team has equal responsibility for the team's defensive depth. In the individual sections (defense, etc.), the relative positions of the players should be adjusted constantly to guarantee depth. The distance between the attacking and midfield sections can be varied so that when the forward player is under pressure, the player farther back reacts. When the ball is played out to the wing, for example, the player farther back moves back down the pitch. The same principle applies to adjustment of the relative distance between a midfielder and a player at the rear of the attacking lineup.

The players should become used to knowing the positions of their nearest teammates and to judging when a deep position is appropriate. A defender behind a teammate who is pressuring the player with the ball should quickly take up a supporting position in order to back up and prevent exploitation of the free area behind the pressuring player. A defender farther from the ball should judge whether the positions of team members who are behind and closer to the ball ensure that the area has depth. If not, the defender should edge toward the area around the ball by backing diagonally, to capture a deep pass or fill a free area. Communication between players is vital if these disparate actions are to succeed as a whole. The individual players should always know how their teammates are trying to create an effective defensive game.

A defender will be outnumbered several times during the course of a game. To maintain depth on defense, the player must move back in a way that forces the two attackers to pass to each other and does not allow a deep pass. The distance between the defender and the player with the ball should prevent the latter from moving up at speed and should invite the attacker to play to a teammate. The distance should be adjusted so that if a pass is made to the teammate, the defender can quickly take up a new, correct defensive position. In this situation, the defender should constantly face the pair of opponents. The defender may therefore undertake what is called "sliding," that is, moving slightly to one side with short, light steps. In this way, the defender creates time for other defenders to come and help out. The defender should be patient and not gamble on winning the ball.

Practices and Drills

We have provided a range of drills for practicing depth in defensive play. The first drill (Defensive Depth Warm-Up) can be used as a warm-up exercise.

Defensive Depth Warm-Up

Players

Six.

Description

Player 1 passes diagonally to 2 while 3 runs deep behind 2. Player 2 lets the ball run past, and 3 takes it. Player 3 likewise passes to 4 while 5 runs deep behind 4. Player 4 lets the ball run past, and 5 takes it. Player 5 passes diagonally to 6 while 2 runs deep behind 6. Player 6 lets the ball run past, and 2 takes it. See figure 8.1. Player 2 passes to 1 while 4 runs deep behind 1, and so on.

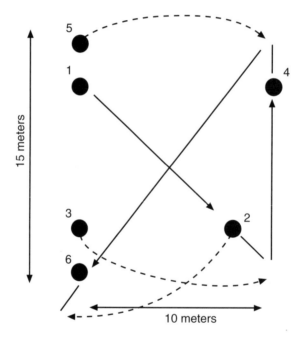

Figure 8.1 Defensive depth warm-up.

Coordinating Defensive Depth

Pitch

Approximately one quarter of the pitch, consisting of three zones (1-3) and one large goal.

Players

Eight: four attackers (black team), three defenders, and a goalkeeper (white team).

Organization

One black-team player (4) is in zone 1, with the rest of the players starting in zone 2, as shown in figure 8.2.

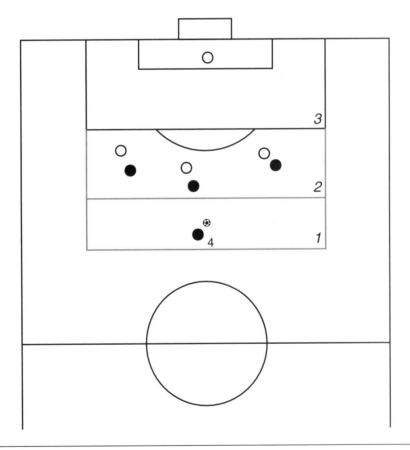

Figure 8.2 Coordinating defensive depth.

Description

Normal game.

Conditions

Player 4 is restricted to zone 1. The rest of the players are restricted to zone 2, except that attackers may dribble into zone 3, where they should finish after dribbling.

Scoring

The black team scores in the large goal, while the white team scores by passing to 4 in zone 1.

Variations

1. After serving, 4 may join the others in zone 2. The white team scores by playing the goalkeeper, who should put the ball up into the center circle.
2. The players can go anywhere on the pitch. The offside rule is in force.
3. An extra white-team player (sweeper) is added. This player may go only into zone 3.

Coaching Points

In this exercise, the three white-team players will practice creating depth in defensive play. You should focus on the two players who are not pressuring the player with the ball. One can act as a backup player. The other should take up a position that provides an overview of the game situation as a whole.

In variation one, greater pressure is put on the white team because it is outnumbered. It is even more important for the defender farthest from the ball to take up a deep position, which will enable this player to evaluate the game situation and back up if necessary.

Variation two enables the white team to exploit the offside rule as part of its tactics for the deep defender.

In variation three, it is important to highlight the distance between the sweeper and the forward defensive players. Communication between these players is particularly important—players should understand how the sweeper can direct and guide the others.

Keywords

Support • Orientation • Judge • Communication • Sideways movement

Zone Depth

Pitch

Approximately one eighth of the pitch, divided into three zones (1-3).

Players

Four: two defenders (2 and 3) and two attackers.

Organization

The attackers start with the ball outside zone 1. Player 2 is in zone 1 and player 3 is in zone 3. See figure 8.3.

Conditions

Player 2 may defend only in zones 1 and 2, while player 3 may defend only in zones 2 and 3.

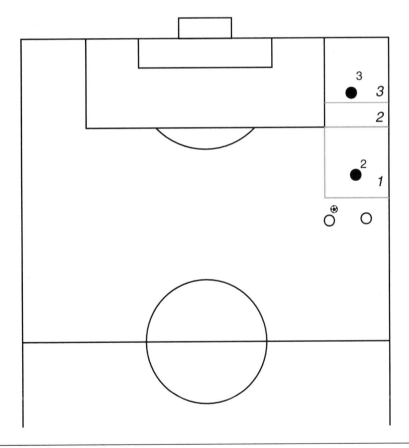

Figure 8.3 Zone depth.

Description

The attackers dribble or play the ball into zone 1, and player 2 should prevent them from getting through to zone 3. If they do, player 3 takes over the defensive role and should prevent the attackers from dribbling the ball over the opposite goal line.

Scoring

The attackers score points by dribbling the ball across the opposite goal line, while the defenders score points by winning and maintaining possession. If the ball is won in zones 1 or 2, the attackers start again at the beginning.

Variations

1. The pitch is widened.
2. Player 2 may also go into zone 3 when the ball is played into that area.

Coaching Points

This exercise focuses on situations in which a defender is outnumbered. It is important for 2 to be patient and work with "sliding" movements. As the attackers approach zone 2, player 2 should try to maneuver them into a position that will enable 3 to participate—and in which the ball can be won, perhaps by pressuring the player with the ball out to the sideline. Player 3 should judge the development of the game and decide where and when it is best to intervene. If the attackers play past 2, player 3 should quickly pressure the player with the ball to increase the chances of an error.

In variation one it becomes easier for the attackers to play past 2 and 3. This means that 2 and 3 must get into the correct defensive positions more quickly, and their "sliding" movements should be effective.

Variation two sets the scene for tighter coordination between the two defenders. Player 2 will find it easier to lay the foundations for regaining possession by directing the player with the ball to one side and refraining from pressuring until the ball is close to zone 2. Player 3 should guide and direct 2 with regard to his or her own position. Player 2, if outplayed, should move back behind 3.

Keywords

Support • Orientation • Judge • Communication • Sideways movement

Creating Depth

Pitch

Approximately one third of the pitch, divided into four zones (1-4) with one large goal.

Players

Eleven: The white team consists of a server (3), three midfielders (7, 8, and 10), and a striker (11). The black team consists of three midfielders (3, 6, and 9), two defenders (4 and 5), and a goalkeeper (1).

Organization

Both teams are organized in two sections. White 3 is behind the centerline. White 7, 8, and 10 are together with black 3, 6, and 9 in zone 1. Black 4 and 5 are in zones 2 and 3 respectively, while white 11 may go into zones 2 and 3. See figure 8.4.

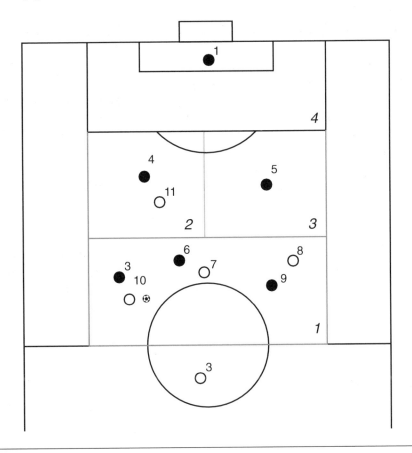

Figure 8.4   Creating depth.

Description

The game starts when 3 passes to 7, 8, or 10, after which 3 may participate as a passing option for the white team.

Conditions

The players should remain in their zones. The white-team player who passes to white 11 may go into zones 2 and 3.

Scoring

The white team scores in the large goal after dribbling into the penalty area (zone 4). The black team scores by playing white 3 in the center circle.

Variations

1. A white-team player other than the one passing to 11 may go into zones 2 and 3.

2. Once the ball has been played into zone 2 or 3, all restrictions are lifted.

Coaching Points

This game should help the black-team players to understand how depth in defense is created. Players 4 and 5 have to think about the distance between themselves and the forward section in conjunction with the game situation and the position of the white team. The three-player section (3, 6, and 9) should consider how to create opportunities for pressure and reinforcement.

Variation one will make the game less predictable for the black team, increasing the need for communication among the defenders. This is also the case in variation two, which will call for more defensive principles, such as reinforcement and recovery.

Keywords

Support • Orientation • Judge • Communication • Sideways movement

CHAPTER 9

Cohesion Between Lines

A good team acts as a compact unit when defending. The different team sections maintain a short distance between one another (see figure 9.1). This enables them to pressure the player with the ball quickly, set up reinforcements, and move several players across toward the ball. If a team can establish this compact unit quickly, it can also make conscious use of the offside trap as a defensive weapon. This compact unit is sometimes visible in aerial television pictures immediately before a goal kick. The players are gathered on approximately one third of the pitch. Situations will sometimes arise when players, particularly those on the attacking team, are spread over a larger area. If the team loses the ball, players must immediately try to unite and move lots of players to the goal side of the ball (see figure 9.2 on page 159). If gaping holes appear between the different sections, the opposition will exploit them, and it may be difficult for a team to gain the time and overview necessary to correct the imbalance.

Goals

- To leave the smallest possible space for the opposition's game when the opponent has the ball.
- To be close to opponents around the ball.
- To have both width and depth in the area around the ball.

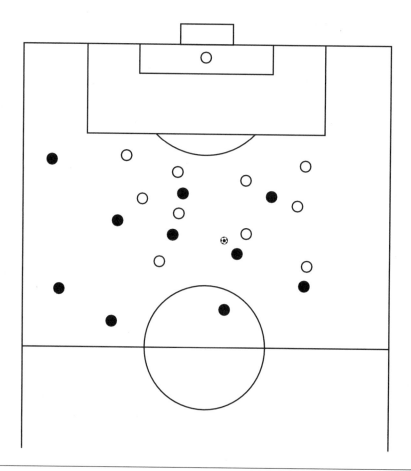

Figure 9.1   A team acts as a compact unit by maintaining short distances between sections.

Coordination Fundamentals

Every player on a team should participate in and feel responsible for coordinating the different team sections. This coordination is partly created by maintaining a certain distance between the vertical lines and partly by sideways movements (see figure 9.2). When lines move, the effect should be that of an elastic unit in which the movements of one section immediately pull the others with it, ensuring that the distance between them does not increase substantially. We talk about teams "making the pitch smaller," which means that they limit the playing area available to the opposition. The players should feel as if they are attached by elastic to each other. As the ball is traveling toward the opposition's penalty area, for instance, the midfield moves up toward the attacking area, simultaneously pulling the defense forward on the pitch so that the team remains a compact unit through the centerline right up to the opposition's penalty area. This direction of movement reverses when the

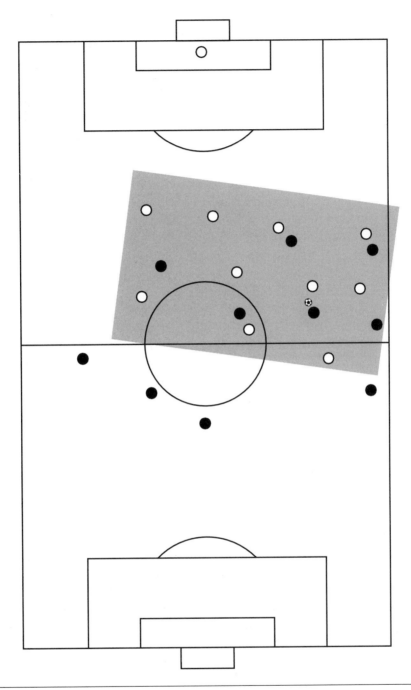

Figure 9.2 If the players are too spread out, they will have to quickly unite into a smaller area to defend if they lose the ball.

opposition plays a ball across the centerline. The midfield should now move closer to the defense, while the attacking section automatically moves closer to the team's own goal. It is not only forward movements that require and create unity, but also sideways movements, in which the wide player either pulls the line if the ball is on that side or is pulled in the opposite direction when the ball is farthest away. Sideways movements are important in creating the compact unit. The movements of individual players are based on the basic principles of individual defensive action (see chapter 1).

When practicing this coordination of sections, players should become used to orienting themselves to their teammates' positions. They should also learn the kinds of situations in which they need to communicate with teammates to maintain the correct distance between one another.

Practices

On the following pages, we have provided some exercises for practicing coordination between team sections.

Elastic Connection

Pitch

One quarter of the pitch, divided into 12 fields, as shown in figure 9.3.

Players

Ten: five versus five.

Description

One team has constant possession of the ball for 10 minutes. The game has two 10-minute halves. If the ball is won, or when a goal is scored, the attacking team starts again behind its own goal line.

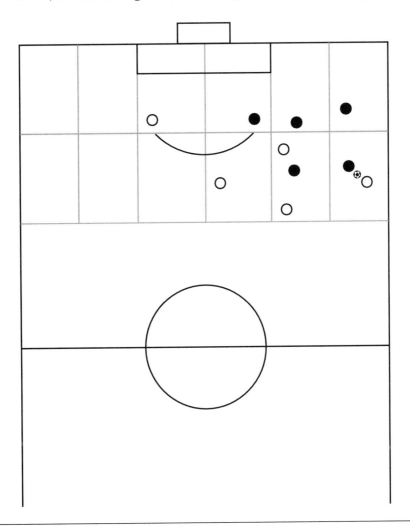

Figure 9.3 Elastic connection.

Conditions

The players on each team should be in adjacent areas. A one-player offside rule is in force.

Scoring

The attacking team scores by dribbling the ball over the defending team's goal line.

Variations

1. The game continues when the ball is won, and both teams score by dribbling over the opposite goal line, the condition being that the ball has previously been in the row of zones closest to the team's own goal line.

2. Each team has one extra player who is behind the row of zones. This player functions as a passing point.

Coaching Points

This exercise should give defenders experience in maintaining an awareness of the positions of their teammates while quickly forming a compact unit. If one defender moves, this will affect the others, who will feel the effect of the "elastic." By taking up a position behind the goal line, you can guide the defense and let them know when they are not a compact unit.

In variation one, teams will have to switch between attacking and defending. This means that defenders must learn to find their positions quickly in order to create a compact unit. This starts with the player closest to the opponent with the ball, whose position determines the areas the others should use to create a block.

Use of the back player in variation two will cause the playing areas to change frequently. This increases the pressure on the defending team's ability to switch to defense and maintain a compact unit.

Keywords

Consistent distance • Sideways movement • Elastic unit • Compact • Orientation • Communication • Make the pitch smaller

Maintaining the Connection

Pitch

Approximately three quarters of the pitch, divided into four zones (1-4) with two large goals, as shown in figure 9.4.

Players

Eighteen: eight versus eight, plus a goalkeeper on each team.

Description

Normal game.

Conditions

A team may only be distributed across two adjacent zones (with the exception of the goalkeeper).

Scoring

As normal.

Variations

1. An extra player joins in—a joker who is always on the side of the team with the ball.
2. The number of zones can be increased to, say, six.

Coaching Points

The idea of this exercise is to prevent gaping holes from opening up between a team's defense, midfield, and attacking sections. The players get used to noting the positions of their teammates and to ensuring that the team makes the pitch as small as possible. In the transition from attack to defense when the team loses the ball, the opponent with the ball should be pressured, and the remaining players should take up appropriate defensive positions.

In variation one, the defensive team faces more pressure, increasing the need for quick organization of the defense.

Variation two can be introduced if the players are having difficulty in implementing the move from one zone to the next.

Keywords

Consistent distance • Sideways movement • Elastic unit • Compact • Orientation • Communication • Make the pitch smaller

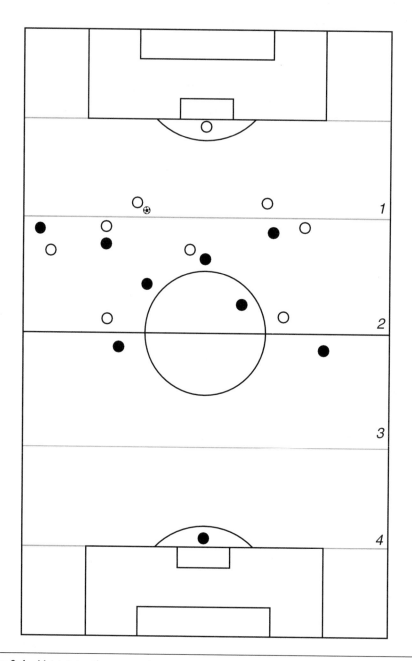

Figure 9.4 Maintaining the connection.

CHAPTER 10

Goalkeeper Responsibilities

The main task of the goalkeeper in defensive play is to reduce the opposition's chances of scoring. This task is not carried out just on the basis of the goalkeeper's technique and personality, but also using the experience and routines developed in training with other players. When the opposition has the ball, the goalkeeper should actively participate in the organization, direction, and supervision of the defense.

Supervision

As the defender at the rear, the goalkeeper has the entire game ahead and in view and therefore has a good opportunity to guide teammates. This player can provide information about the movements of opponents between or over the defensive line, thereby increasing the defenders' awareness of those who are out of their field of vision. At the same time, this guidance also serves as a kind of locator on the goalkeeper's position in the defensive area. When getting involved in the game out on the field—moving out to intercept a cross, for example—the goalkeeper's information to players should be based on previously rehearsed and agreed-on moves. A defender might move in a particular way, for example, when the goalkeeper calls, "Mine."

It is the responsibility of the goalkeeper to position the players in the last third of the pitch in dead-ball situations (see *Soccer Systems & Strategies,* page 129). At these times, players should be positioned so that the goalkeeper has the best possible space for intervention. There is often a tendency for defenders to move in too close to goal, overcrowding the area.

Position

The goalkeeper should take up a position relative to the ball. If the ball is deep in the opposition's half, the goalkeeper should stand a little outside the penalty area to capture long balls into the defensive half of the pitch. When the goalkeeper's team is working with high pressure, the proper move is forward into a position as an extra sweeper. The Danish national

Anyone can see that Peter Schmeichel directs his defenders. Throughout his international career, the information he has given to his teammates has been a vital factor in Denmark's strong defense.

goalkeeper has often demonstrated exactly how decisive this position can be—such as during the team's international breakthrough at the 1984 European Championships. In the final qualifier against Belgium, Ole Qvist ran right outside the penalty area and tackled a Belgian player who was free after the failure of the Danish offside trap. Qvist's intervention prevented the Belgians winning 3-1, which would undoubtedly have put Denmark out of the European Championships. Since then, Peter Schmeichel has filled this extra sweeper position successfully for both Denmark and Manchester United.

When play is in the defensive half of the pitch, the goalkeeper should be ready to meet a ball played deep past the defense. The goalkeeper should, however, not be tempted too far out of goal, where a long lob might cause problems. Too often, we see a good shooter fire a surprise long shot into the back of the net while the goalkeeper desperately scrambles backward in an attempt to stop it. Use the following drill (on pages 168 to 169) to practice the goalkeeper's responsibilities and interaction with teammates in defensive situations.

Keeper Scoop-Up

Pitch

Approximately one half of the pitch, divided into two zones (1 and 2), with one large goal and two smaller ones, as shown in figure 10.1.

Players

Eleven: five versus five and a goalkeeper.

Description

Normal game.

Conditions

The white team can only score once the ball has been played from zone 2 into zone 1. No player may go into zone 1 until the ball has been passed there. The black team has no restrictions.

Variations

1. A limited number of touches is imposed—a maximum of two touches, say, for the white team.
2. Passes into zone 1 must be in the air.

Coaching Points

This game trains the goalkeeper's ability to move out and snap up those deep passes. In each game situation, the goalkeeper should decide whether to stay in the goal or come out. This player should consider the chances of teammates preventing a shot and can coordinate with them by directing them into positions to reduce the finishing angle, limiting his or her own choice of position.

In variation one, several situations will arise in which the white team will play the ball into zone 1.

Variation two will give the goalkeeper more time, but it will be more difficult to play the ball on if he is outside the penalty area.

Keywords

Guidance • Position

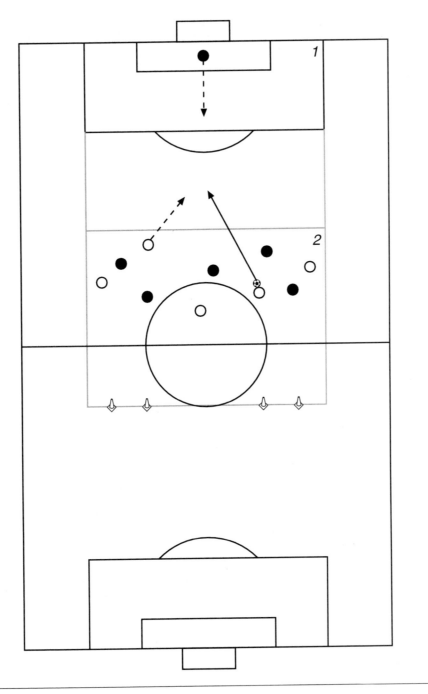

Figure 10.1 Keeper scoop-up.

CHAPTER 11

High-Pressure Attack

We have explained the different principles of defensive organization and provided suggestions for coaching the defensive game. Even if two teams are using the same defensive organization, however, there can be great differences in the way they perform their defensive tasks. In team tactics, for example, the team can decide to move back down into its own half of the pitch before establishing the defense—or do the opposite, and on losing the ball immediately try to regain it. The ratio between offensive and defensive defense produces different types of defensive styles, as described in *Soccer Systems & Strategies*. Among the most common are pressure play, catenaccio, and its own particular defensive variant, offside trap. We discuss pressure play in this chapter, offside trap in chapter 12, and catenaccio in chapter 13.

The Principle of Pressure Play

The main principle of pressure play is that the defending team establishes systematic, intensive cover around the ball and places a lot of pressure on the player in possession.

If a defending team can create a situation in which it is equal to or greater in number than the attackers near the ball, it has a greater chance of regaining possession. There are many situations in which teams can create an opportunity for defenders to equal or outnumber attackers—for instance, when an opponent receives a pass in a "closed" area, such as down the sideline, where freedom of movement is limited, or if the attacker receives a poor pass or a high ball that will require some time to control.

One player can shape a team's defensive style. Lothar Matthäus, the German striker, lent both an offensive and defensive dimension to his team's defensive game. His ability to see the game made him a far-sighted defender, and when he won the ball, he ignited the attack.

The same applies in an area containing many players, which makes it harder for the player with the ball to get an overview of the game situation and therefore demands more time to adapt to it. Some teams have developed a style of play based on pressuring the player with the ball quickly and directly while other nearby team members "close" the area. This defensive style has earned the name "pressure soccer," and during the 1990s, with the Brøndby Super League team leading the way, it became a dominant method of regaining the ball in Danish soccer. Teams also vary when and how to apply pressure. We talk about teams applying high pressure, where they try to quickly establish their pressure play deep in the opposing half, while other teams use low pressure, which means that they intervene in their own half. High pressure is an important part of the "direct" style of play, as described in *Soccer Systems & Strategies*.

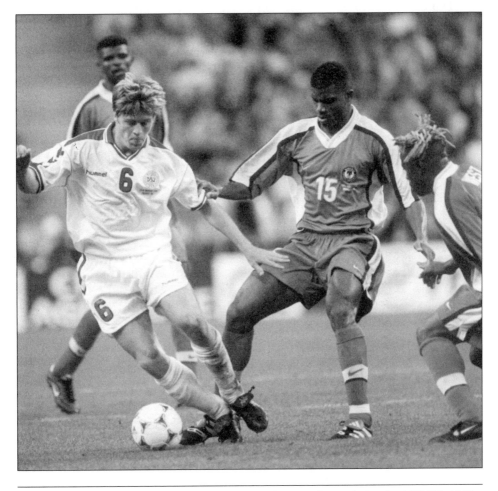

Thomas Helveg comes under pressure from three Nigerian players during the 1998 World Cup quarterfinal. Oliseh is pressuring Helveg from the front and West from the side.

Goals

- To reduce space and passing options for the player with the ball.
- To increase the chance of the player with the ball making a mistake, and therefore the defensive team's chance of regaining the ball.
- To have many passing options in the transition to quick forward play when the ball is regained.
- To surprise the opposition.

Pressure Fundamentals

If pressure play is to be effective, the defending players must quickly get into their covering positions around the ball. When a team applies pressure, the players involved should move forward or sideways while a backup is established (see figure 11.1). While the ball is on its way toward white 5, black 2 breaks toward 5 (forward-directed). Black 6 also moves forward by breaking toward the area around black 2, while black 7 and 4 both break toward the area around the ball (side-oriented). Black 6 takes up a backup position for black 2, while black 10 stands in line with the player in possession of the ball to prevent a pass to the side. In order for the pressure to cause problems for the opposition, players must move quickly and in a coordinated manner.

Black 2 starts the pressure play in figure 11.1 by pressuring the player with the ball, while other teammates pressure the nearest passing options. Coordination is vital, since the primary aim of the pressure on the player with the ball is to force a poor pass, which the other defenders can snap up. The player pressuring the ball should not simply concentrate on winning the ball but should also attempt to force a pass into an area containing many defending teammates and should impede this pass, so that the intended recipient cannot easily control or play the ball.

Figure 11.2 shows a situation in which white 2 receives the ball from the goalkeeper. While the ball is traveling toward 2, black 10 moves toward white 2 to pressure him or her as the player with the ball. As 10 makes this run, the rest of the black-team players in the area move into positions giving them a chance of regaining the ball in the event of a poor pass from white 2. Note that this means white 11, farthest away from the area around the ball, will not be covered.

The player who first pressures the player with the ball is defender number 1. The player behind defender number1 is defender number 2, who reinforces 1. The next few players close to the area around the ball are called number 3 defenders. The functions of these closer players are described in the following section.

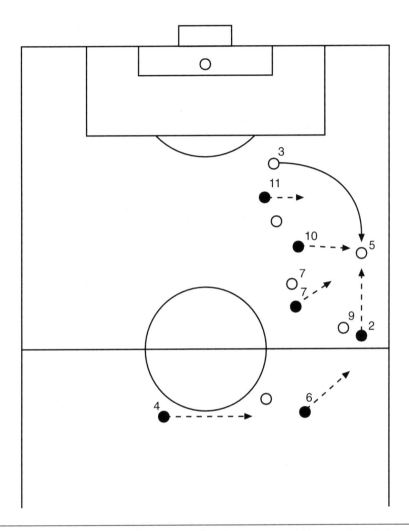

Figure 11.1 To achieve successful pressure play, players must quickly move into their covering positions around the ball, as the black team does here.

Main Points for Defender Number 1

Judgment. The player should judge when it is appropriate to apply pressure. Certain game situations can automatically signal a need to apply pressure. Generally speaking, it is the movements of defender number 1 that pull the other defenders into the pressure, but sometimes a call from a "director"—a guiding player farther back who has a good view of the possibilities for other players to create effective pressure—can send defender number 1 into pressuring action.

Change of tempo. A player who has decided to apply pressure should take action quickly and decisively. Pressure should start while the ball is

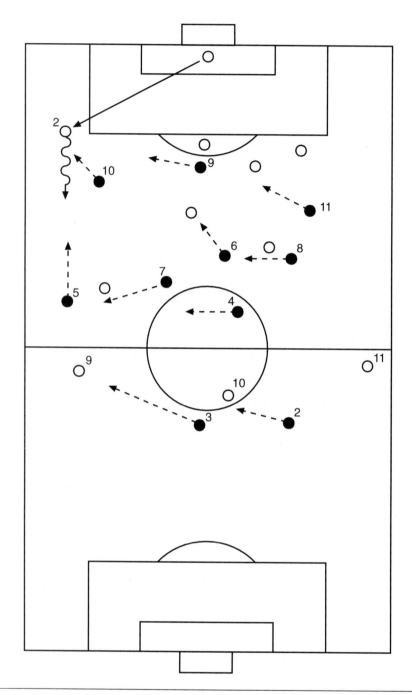

Figure 11.2 Here the black-team players move into positions conducive to regaining the ball if white 2 makes a weak pass.

traveling toward the new player. This is partly because it will disturb this player's observation, and partly because it will reduce the time the attacker has to work with the ball.

Pressuring position. At the instant the receiving player makes contact with the ball, defender number 1 should get into the correct defensive position—slightly sideways, with knees bent—and be ready to either win the ball or close down certain passing angles. The defender should not make this obvious, instead reducing the tempo while approaching the player with the ball. Otherwise, the defender risks being passed easily.

Main Point for Defender Number 2

Reinforcement. This player should move forward and back up the number 1 defender, even if this means leaving an opponent. He or she should take up a position allowing the number 1 defender to pay full attention to pressuring the player with the ball.

Main Points for the Number 3 Defenders

Close up. Team members in the area should close up as defender number 1 moves to apply pressure. That is, players should quickly move toward the player with the ball and take up positions to support defender number 1's pressure as far as possible.

Side-oriented. At least one player should quickly undertake to screen one of the horizontal passing options from the player with the ball. If the pressure takes place close to one of the sidelines, the only remaining passing option will be backward.

Teammates who are farther away from the ball should move toward the area around it so they can quickly get into good defensive positions if the opponent completes a pass. The players should create the required compact organization.

Forward-directed. The team members around the ball should quickly move up to their nearest opponents and mark them tightly. From this position, they should either snap up a weak pass or take up a new position if the ball is played on.

Communication

Coordination of the players' movements requires good communication within the team. During training and noncompetitive games, you, as coach, should practice calling to initiate pressure and incite the right level of aggression. The call, "Go!" can, for example, be used as a signal to begin pressure play, followed by, "Close up!" Teams that work best together have no need for these vocal commands. At a glance, the players use their experience and read situations in which they can use pressure play.

Timing

Because pressure play is physically demanding, it is a good idea to use it only at certain times during a game. Teams should therefore work at finding and agreeing on game situations when pressure play has the greatest chance of success.

Practices and Drills

We have provided a list of drills and games you can use when practicing pressure play. In these exercises, you should look at the work of defenders numbers 1 and 2 in context. The first drill can be used as a warm-up exercise.

Outnumbered

Pitch

One third of the pitch between the centerline and the penalty area.

Players

Fifteen: three teams (A, B, and C) of five players.

Description

Two teams (10 players) play against one team (five players)—teams A and B against C, for example. When a player from the smaller team (C) touches the ball, the teams rotate, so that C now plays with A or B, depending on which team made the error enabling team C to touch the ball. You should announce the outnumbered team. A maximum of two touches is allowed. See figure 11.3.

Variations

1. The number of players and pitch size can be increased or decreased.

2. The game is played with two balls. If one ball is touched, the other ball is also affected; that is, both balls move into the possession of another team.

3. There are no restrictions on touches.

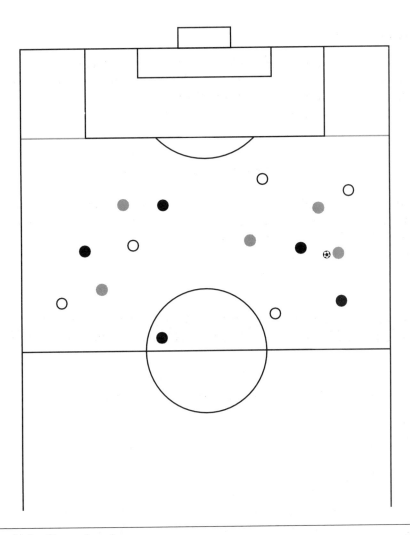

Figure 11.3   Outnumbered.

Coaching Points

The relatively large pitch forces the outnumbered team to coordinate when applying pressure. The team should identify times when it is easier to apply coordinated pressure. Likewise, a team must gain experience in switching from being the team with the ball to being the team seeking to regain the ball.

Anticipation

Pitch

One half of the pitch with two large goals.

Players

Twelve: six versus four and two goalkeepers.

Organization

The white team plays with three at the back (2, 3, and 5) and one player as a defensive midfielder (6). The black team plays with two strikers (10 and 11), two midfielders (8 and 9), and two wingbacks (2 and 5). See figure 11.4.

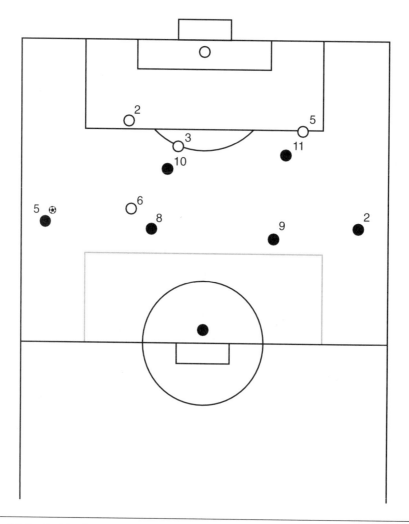

Figure 11.4   Anticipation.

Description

The goalkeeper on the black team starts by playing either 8 or 9. The white team should, on winning the ball, play another teammate, who may have no more than three touches before attempting a long shot.

Scoring

As normal.

Variations

1. Another midfielder joins each team.
2. The playing arena is extended to cover three quarters of a full-size pitch, while the white team has two strikers and another player at the back (i.e., the team is playing four at the back).
3. A joker is added and is always on the side of the team with the ball. This player should stay close to the sidelines to create width and is allowed a maximum of two touches.

Coaching Points

The aim of this exercise is for the three players performing zonal cover at the back to win the ball early by positioning their defensive line well forward on the pitch.

This will emphasize sideways movements combined with a forward defensive line. The defensive midfielder's efforts to pressure the opposition's passes in a certain direction determine the direction of movement. You should impress upon the players that defensive movements are determined by the teammate next in line.

Variations one and two highlight the dependency between the midfielders and the players at the back.

Variation three introduces a joker who, due to a fixed position on the wing, can increase the breadth of the game and put more pressure on the sideways movements of the defense. The game now changes constantly, and these transitional phases are critical, giving players an understanding of the establishment of the defensive lines. You should pay particular attention to the quick forward break by the defense after winning the ball and forward play.

You and your players should bear in mind the basic rules of defense.

Keywords

Defender number 1: Judgment • Change of tempo • Pressure position
Defender number 2: Support
Number 3 defenders: Close up • Sideways-oriented • Forward-directed
General: Communication • Timing

Central Pressure

Pitch

Approximately two fifths of the pitch from the penalty area to the centerline, with one large goal.

Players

Thirteen: eight on the black team (2, 3, 4, 5, 6, 7, 10, and a goalkeeper) and five on the white team (7, 8, 9, 10, and 11).

Organization

White 7 is in the center circle closest to the goal, while black 10 is in the other half of the center circle.

Description

White 8 starts by playing white 7, after which play is unrestricted. See figure 11.5.

Scoring

The white team scores in the large goal. The black team scores one point after five passes between team members without losing the ball.

Variation

Play on one half of the full pitch. Another player is added to each team. Both new players should start in the center circle.

Coaching Points

This exercise focuses on applying pressure when the opposition establishes play around the center of the pitch. Black 10 should quickly try to make contact with white 7 and should take up a position on the wing from which he can participate in horizontal pressure in relation to the midfield pressure and sideways movement.

If white 7 dribbles to the left, black 5 should pressure immediately while 6 and 7 move sideways. Black 10 should apply horizontal pressure in relation to the position of black 5. Black 10 should judge whether black 5 is opening toward the side or toward the center. Coordination between the team members at the front and the pressuring midfielders is particularly important.

In the variation, the pitch's size becomes more realistic, making it more physically demanding.

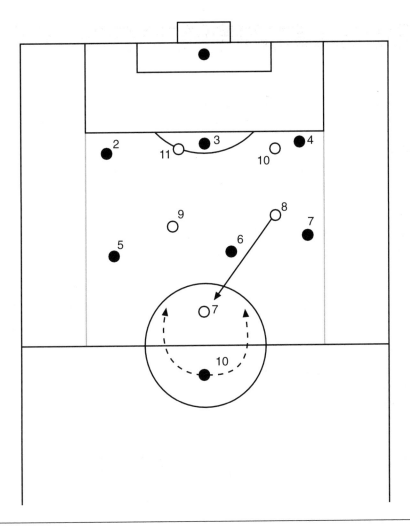

Figure 11.5   Central pressure.

Keywords

Defender number 1: Judgment • Change of tempo • Pressure position

Defender number 2: Support

Number 3 defenders: Close up • Sideways-oriented • Forward-directed

General: Communication • Timing

Distributing Pressure Tasks

Pitch

One quarter of the pitch, with a center zone (2) and two wing zones (1 and 3), as shown in figure 11.6.

Players

Sixteen: eight versus eight.

Organization

Four black-team and two white-team players are in zones 1 and 3. Four white-team players are in zone 2. The four white-team players in zone 2 work in pairs.

Description

The black team starts in zone 1 by passing to zone 3, at which point two white-team players from zone 2 may move in while the pass is on its way. These two white-team players, together with their team-mates, should establish pressure in this zone (3). If the black team plays the ball to zone 1, the other two white-team players move from zone 2 into zone 1, while the two white-team players from zone 3 move back into zone 2.

Scoring

The black team scores when it manages three passes between zones 1 and 3 without the white-team players winning the ball.

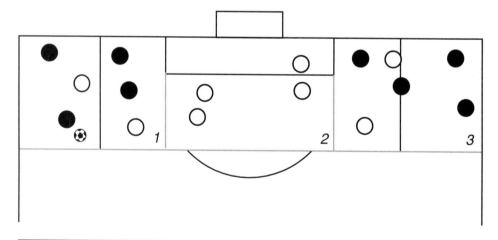

Figure 11.6   Distributing pressure tasks.

Conditions

Two-touch play.

Variations

1. Only the player receiving the ball must take two touches.
2. There are no restrictions on touches.
3. The pitch is made longer and narrower.
4. There are no limitations on the number of players from zone 2 who can move into one of the wing zones.

Coaching Points

This game places particular importance on the ability of the white team to quickly decide how to distribute the pressuring tasks among the four players in the zone. The two players already in the zone will usually be defenders numbers 1 and 3, while the two approaching players take up positions in relation to those of their teammates. It will then be possible to establish defenders numbers 1, 2, and 3 in the zone. The game in the wing zone will always require pressure tasks to be changed around, forcing the white-team players to switch defensive tasks on an ongoing basis.

Variations one and two enable the team with the ball to raise the tempo of the game, making the task of defending more difficult.

Variation three presents an opportunity for practicing applying pressure near the sidelines.

Variation four gives the white team the option of introducing as many defenders as the players think necessary to have the best chance of winning the ball in that particular game situation.

Keywords

Defender number 1: Judgment • Change of tempo • Pressure position
Defender number 2: Support
Number 3 defenders: Close up • Sideways-oriented • Forward-directed
General: Communication • Timing

Pressure Play

Pitch

Approximately one quarter of the pitch divided into two zones (1 and 2), with one large goal and two smaller ones using four cones on each baseline. See figure 11.7 for the setup.

Players

Nine: four versus four, and a goalkeeper.

Organization

Each team has two players in each zone.

Description

Normal game; the white team attacks the two smaller goals.

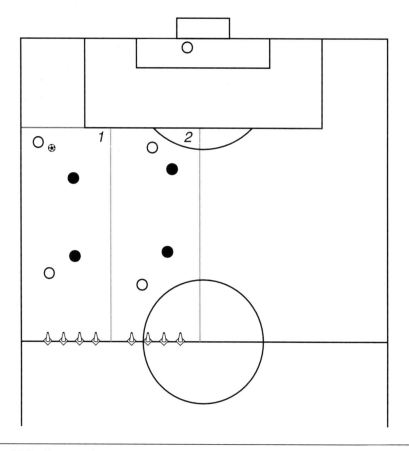

Figure 11.7 Pressure play.

Conditions

The black-team players may not leave their zones while the white team has the ball. The goalkeeper may only put the ball into play by throwing to one of the two closest white-team players. The ball cannot be played back to the goalkeeper.

Scoring

The black team scores in the large goal. The white team scores by knocking over one or more cones. Each cone knocked over counts as one point.

Variations

1. Another player is added to the white team. He or she should always be the playmaker at the back. He or she should receive the ball from the goalkeeper and direct the play.
2. The pitch is extended lengthwise.

Coaching Points

This game enables the black team to practice high pressure. The focus is on the two important types of movement involved in pressure play: the forward movements of defender number 1 and the support player (defender number 2), and the sideways movements of the other two defenders.

Variation one will create several situations where the upfield play area is changed, causing more transition scenarios for the black team.

Variation two increases the distance between the players, thus increasing the importance of timing in pressure play.

Keywords

Defender number 1: Judgment • Change of tempo • Pressure position
Defender number 2: Support
Number 3 defenders: Close up • Sideways-oriented • Forward-directed
General: Communication • Timing

Initiating Pressure

Pitch

One half of the pitch with three small goals on both goal lines, as shown in figure 11.8.

Players

Sixteen: eight versus eight.

Description

Normal game, with the offside rule.

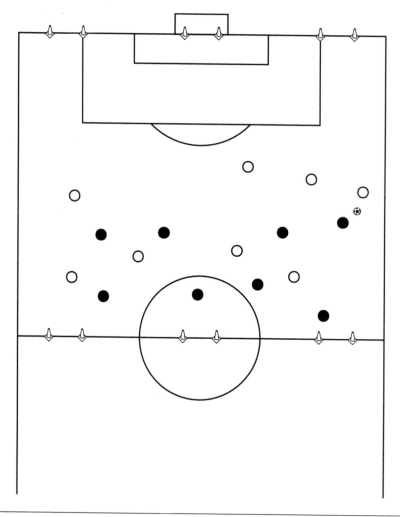

Figure 11.8   Initiating pressure.

Conditions

The starting formation for both teams is 4-4 using zonal cover. The players should play with at least two touches.

Scoring

Goals are scored in the three goals.

Variations

1. There are no restrictions on touches.
2. Fixed scoring conditions are established—for example, alternating between the outer and center goals.

Coaching Points

This game trains the two sections to coordinate in establishing pressure. The players should coordinate the forward movements of defenders numbers 1 and 2, and the sideways movements of the other defenders. By pushing the game out to the sidelines, the team will find it easier to establish pressure play. Likewise, during play down the center of the pitch, the relative distribution of pressuring tasks will come more into focus.

Variation one increases the tempo of the game. It may be necessary to return to the two-touch restriction for a few minutes at a time.

Once a goal has been scored in variation two, you can suggest that the next point may not be scored in a particular goal. This means that the team can only score in two of the three goals. The defensive team can then increase its level of aggressiveness in attempting to regain the ball.

Keywords

Defender number 1: Judgment • Change of tempo • Pressure position
Defender number 2: Support
Number 3 defenders: Close up • Sideways-oriented • Forward-directed
General: Communication • Timing

CHAPTER 12

Offside Trap

The offside trap is an extremely effective weapon on defense, both for winning the ball and for putting opponents in an offside position. The players at the back coordinate to move up the pitch at high speed (see figure 12.1). Many will remember the Danish national side of the 1980s exploiting this principle with great success under the masterly supervision of Morten Olsen. The internationals Frank Arnesen and Søren Lerby were inspired by their coach, Rinus Michels, who, with the Dutch national team of the 1970s, was one of the earliest proponents of this "trap." This encouraged the Danish team to use the technique. Morten Olsen once said: "I was tired of us always giving away so many easy goals. Using the offside trap, we could ensure that our opponents couldn't get into the penalty area, which was where we were making the errors that often cost us goals. We trained for a couple of days, and learned it. The system works in such a way that others can control the defense. The 'trap' worked perfectly several times, for example, when Jan Mølby took over the sweeper position."

The offside trap should be used in moderation. If the opponents realize their danger, it may be better to use this principle only at certain times during a game. In addition, it is not a good idea to use the offside trap unless the referee or linesman is in a position to correctly judge offside situations.

Goals

- To put opponents in an offside position.
- To limit the space and passing options for the player with the ball.
- To win the ball.
- To move opponents away from the team's own goal.

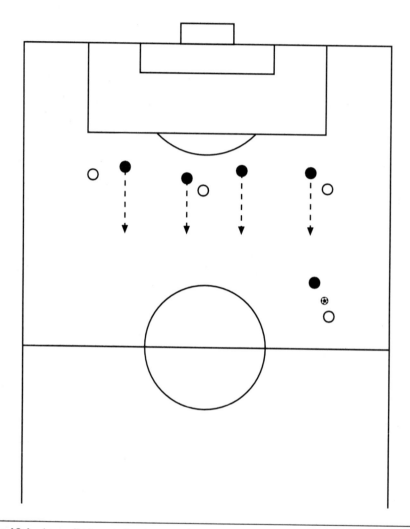

Figure 12.1 In an offside trap, the players at the back coordinate to move up the pitch at high speed.

Offside Trap Fundamentals

The offside trap can typically be used in three situations:

- Under attack from the opposition
- After the ball has been played clear of the team's own goal
- Immediately before the opposition takes a free kick

Following are the general rules for all three situations.

- Put pressure on the player with the ball.
- For the offside trap to succeed, the player with the ball should be allowed no time to weigh options. In a game phase, therefore, one player must quickly pressure the player with the ball. This is usually the player who is closest to the player with the ball.

Organization. A prerequisite of effective offside trap is that all players are in their correct defensive positions. If this is not the case, there is a risk that one or more players will hang back, allowing the opposition to play forward to unmarked attackers.

Director. A player who has an overview of both teammates and the opposition supervises the offside trap. Typically, this is the sweeper.

Signal. The players can rely on a call to signal an offside trap, but the most effective method is for the team to keep an eye on the director while observing situations where such a play can be appropriate. In this way, a player's forward run toward the player with the ball can be a signal to the players to prepare to trap. The director may give a little wave of the hand immediately before the trap is to be established.

Tempo. All the players at the back should run forward as fast as possible. Players should have no doubt in their minds as to the success of the offside trap.

Counter-running player. It is a good idea to have one player— typically an offensive midfielder or an attacker—moving back toward his or her own goal while the team is using the offside trap. This player can intervene if the trap goes wrong. The counter-running player must be careful to avoid getting far enough down the pitch to put the players back onside.

Goalkeeper. While the team is using the offside trap, the goalkeeper should be toward the edge of the penalty area, ready to intervene if the opposition plays a long ball forward.

Practices and Drills

Following are special drills and exercises for use when practicing the offside trap. Use the first three drills as warm-up exercises.

Offside Trap Warm-Up

Players

Six.

Description

When 1 passes to 2, 3 runs toward 2. Player 2 dribbles toward 3, who should prevent 2 from passing the marked line. Once 2 has passed the line, 2 dribbles back toward 5 and passes to 6. Player 4 passes with another ball to 1, who dribbles down toward 5, who has run forward, and so on. See figure 12.2.

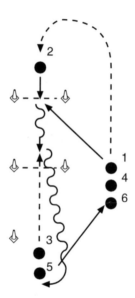

Figure 12.2 Offside trap warm-up.

Director Warm-Up

Pitch

Extended penalty area divided into five zones (1-5).

Players

Eight.

Organization

Five of the players each have a ball and start in zone 3. Five balls each are positioned in zones 1 and 5. See figure 12.3.

Conditions

Players may not go into zones 2 and 4 with a ball.

Description

The players who have a ball dribble around each other, while the three players without a ball try to win one. When a ball is won, the victorious player continues dribbling inside zone 3. One player should be designated the signaler, shouting "Forward!" or "Back!" to direct players to change zones. When this happens, the players should leave the balls where they are. The last three players to reach the new zone have to try to win a ball.

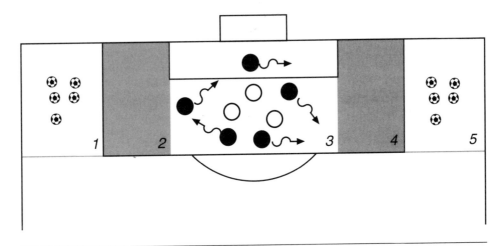

Figure 12.3   Director warm-up.

Tempo Warm-Up

Pitch

Extended penalty area divided into three zones (1-3) with a centerline. See figure 12.4 for the setup.

Players

Six.

Organization

When play commences or after a goal, players should start in their own zones (1 or 3).

Description

To begin, the ball is played in the air from one zone to the opposition's zone. If the ball does not reach the target zone, the opposition gets one point. Otherwise, points are scored when the opposition dribbles the ball across the centerline or when the serving team dribbles into the opposition's zone. After a goal, the scoring team starts with the ball.

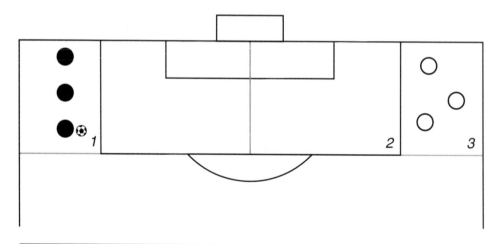

Figure 12.4   Tempo warm-up.

Offside Trap Communication

Pitch

One half of the pitch, divided into two zones (1 and 2) with one large goal.

Players

Fifteen: eight versus seven; the black team consists of five defenders (2-6), two midfielders (7 and 9), and a goalkeeper, and the white team has two attackers, two midfielders, and three defenders.

Organization

Players 2-6 on the black team and the attackers and midfielders from the white team are in zone 1, while the rest of the players are in zone 2. The white team starts with the ball in zone 2. See figure 12.5.

Description

Normal game.

Conditions

The players may not change zones. A one-meter offside rule is in force, so attackers must be more than one meter offside in order to be penalized.

Scoring

The white team scores in the large goal. The black team scores points by playing the ball into the center circle.

Variations

1. The players in zone 2 may also go into zone 1, but not into the penalty area and only when the ball is in zone 2.
2. When the ball is put into zone 2, a free kick is awarded.
3. When the ball is put into zone 1, a corner kick is awarded.

Coaching Points

This game focuses on the coordination between defenders 2-6 while the team is using the offside trap. The trap is controlled by 4, who should time its beginning appropriately. Player 4 should wait until 7 or 9 is pressuring the player with the ball.

The white team should see it as a challenge to avoid going offside and to break through the black team's defense. If the white team is concentrating too much on not being offside, an extra zone can be

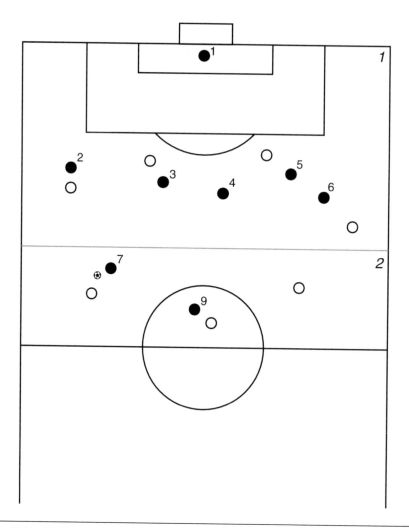

Figure 12.5 Offside trap communication.

inserted between zones 1 and 2 (part of zone 1), into which black 2-6—but not the white-team players from zone 1—may go.

In variation one, either 7 or 9 should run back and cover.

Variation two highlights the offside trap during free kicks. You should focus mainly on the timing of the trap. If it is commenced too early, the opposing players may get the measure of it and turn the situation to their own advantage. If it is begun too late, the opposition's players will not be offside and, furthermore, will have a good chance of breaking free. When the opposition finds a way out, the offside trap technique can be left for a while and then reintroduced.

Variation three will create several corner kicks, enabling you to focus on using the offside trap after a corner kick. When the ball has been cleared from the penalty area, 7 and 9 should pressure the player who has it, giving the defenders time to move forward before the ball is played into the penalty area.

When practicing the offside trap, it is occasionally a good idea for you to take up a position on the defensive line and judge whether the trap is succeeding in putting opponents in an offside position.

Keywords

Pressure the player with the ball • Organization • Supervisor • Signal • Tempo • Counter-running player • Goalkeeper

Training the Counter-Runner

Pitch

One quarter of the pitch, with a centerline and four cones positioned on each goal line, as shown in figure 12.6.

Players

Twelve: six versus six.

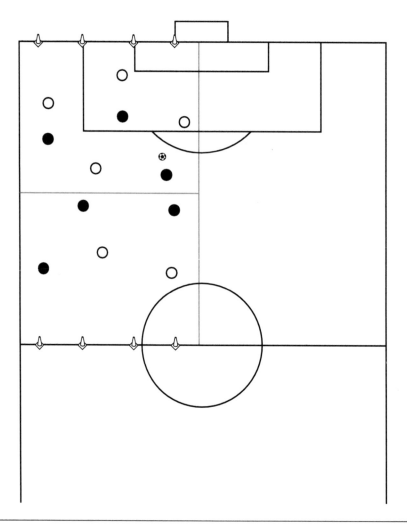

Figure 12.6 Training the counter-runner.

Description

Normal game.

Conditions

When a team plays the ball over the centerline, everyone on the team must have been on the opposition's half of the pitch before any of that team's players may touch the ball in their own half of the pitch. A one-player offside rule is in force.

Scoring

Teams score points by hitting the opposition's cones.

Variation

When the ball has been in the opposition's half of the pitch, only those players who have been over the centerline may touch it in their own half of the pitch.

Coaching Points

In this game, players should become accustomed to running forward quickly and should understand the advantages of moving the rear players quickly up the pitch. If the ball is lost on the opposition's half of the pitch before the players at the back have crossed the centerline, the players close by must pressure the player with the ball to prevent a long pass. In addition, one player (the counter-running player) over the centerline should move back toward his or her own defense to be ready to intercept any long balls. The importance of this counter-running player will become even clearer when the variation is introduced.

Keywords

Pressure the player with the ball • Organization • Supervisor • Signal • Tempo • Counter-running player • Goalkeeper

Pulling Off the Trap

Pitch

Approximately three fifths of the pitch, with two large goals.

Players

Sixteen: eight versus eight, with two attackers, two midfielders, three defenders (two blockers and one sweeper), and a goalkeeper on each team.

Organization

The two attackers and the three defenders on each team are in the same half. See figure 12.7.

Description

Normal game with offside.

Conditions

The defenders and attackers should always stay in the same half of the pitch.

Scoring

As normal.

Variations

1. The ball may not be dribbled over the centerline.
2. When a team wins the ball in its own half, the team may have only three touches before playing it over the centerline.

Coaching Points

This game focuses clearly on coordination between the defenders themselves, and between the defense and midfield, during establishment and implementation of the offside trap. It is a good idea to let players take up their normal team positions. The sweeper controls the initiation of the offside trap and should judge the timing. The defense and midfield players should agree on the "signal." The game enables you to highlight the effects of a premature or belated offside trap. After the defenders have tried the trap a number of times, you can instruct the midfielders as to how they can operate—one at a time—as the counter-running player. When the ball is lost, the attackers must pressure the player who has it.

Variation one gives the defenders further opportunities to use the

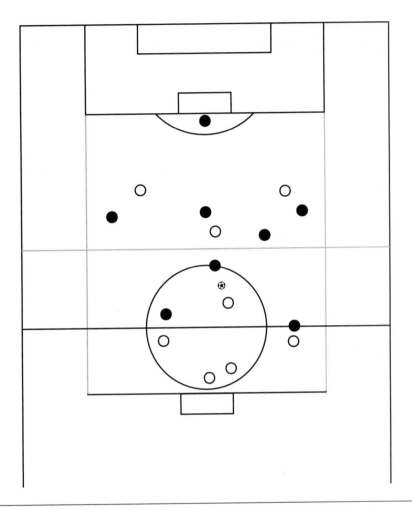

Figure 12.7   Pulling off the trap.

offside trap. The timing of the trap also becomes clearer.

In variation two, the opposition should try to play quickly over the center after winning the ball, enabling the defenders to quickly establish offside trap on losing the ball.

Keywords

Pressure the player with the ball • Organization • Supervisor • Signal • Tempo • Counter-running player • Goalkeeper

CHAPTER 13

Catenaccio

During the late 1950s and early 1960s, Iberian teams Real Madrid and Benfica dominated European tournaments. Their offensive soccer repeatedly won them the Europa Cup.

Milan in 1963 and Inter in 1964 and 1965 succeeded in breaking this run of victories. This was primarily due to a previously unheard-of concentration on defensive safety.

In the mid-1960s, the two Milan clubs, AC Milan and Inter FC, created a school for basic defense. First, both clubs positioned a player behind their four-man defenses as a guard. This defensive formation became known as catenaccio, meaning "bolt" or "lock" in Italian. The task of the player behind the defenders in the back row was to close across if an opponent with the ball broke through the offensive defensive row. Milan and Inter played in a 1-4-3-2 formation, in which the four players at the back of the defensive lineup used a combination of player and zone-based cover.

Inter, whose coach Herrera is the most famous advocate of catenaccio, was particularly successful in fusing the three basic elements perfectly. The primary task was to prevent the opposition from scoring. When Inter positioned the defensive and midfield sections farther down the pitch and placed a free player behind the lines as an extra guard, the opposing team came up against a compact defensive wall that used every means (fair or foul) to prevent goal-scoring opportunities from arising. Next would come a minimal winning goal for Inter, after which the team would concentrate on counterattacking, pushing the opposition forward according to plan. The three midfielders were all sublime passers of the ball, so they could swiftly and precisely play a quickly breaking striker in any gaps that appeared in the opposition's formation. The third factor was a marked shift in situations where the team came forward with a goal. The team adopted a time-consuming style of play that made most of the game crashingly boring.

During the 1960s, Inter's strategy in European tournaments was simple and effective—zero-zero at away games, one-zero at home. This resulted in many boring games, but on the plus side it generally earned the club a place in the final.

Results Soccer

From the point of view of defensive tactics, catenaccio as a style of play is the forerunner of the type of soccer we now call results soccer—that is, a tactic focusing on obtaining a draw (preferably 0-0) or a victory by one goal. The defense takes priority. Since the European club tournaments ordained that, from 1967 onward, goals scored away from home would count double in the event of a draw after two matches, results soccer has been the most commonly used out-pitch tactic in European tournaments.

These kinds of tactical defensive challenges arise for teams at all levels. While some teams use a practiced catenaccio defensive style, others can use the same defensive thinking in particular situations. These may be teams who are facing extremely strong opponents or are working to maintain a lead.

The following exercise may be used for rehearsing the catenaccio style of defense.

Bolt and Lock

Pitch

One half of the pitch, with one large goal and one minigoal.

Players

Fifteen: the black team has eight players, one of whom is a goalkeeper for the first half, against the white team's seven players, with the teams reversing in the second half.

Organization

The black team consists of defenders and midfielders. The white team consists mainly of attackers and midfielders.

Description

This exercise is organized as a game of two halves. The first half has a fixed length of 15 minutes, while the second half can be varied depending on the performance of the black team. The black team begins by attacking the large goal. The result at halftime determines the course of the second half, during which the black team should defend the large goal (see figure 13.1). If, for example, the black team is ahead by one goal and the white team scores one goal in the second half, a further five minutes of playing time is added to the original 15. If the white team scores another goal, another five minutes is added, and so on. If the black team scores, the playing time is reduced by 15 minutes; however, the second half must be at least 15 minutes long. If the black team is ahead or if the score is equal by the time the game is over, the black team is the winner.

Conditions

The team attacking the large goal plays with the offside rule. In the second half, the white numbers 2 and 3 may score with long shots (i.e., from outside the penalty area). The goalkeeper and one player on the black team should change over to the white team at halftime. The first player to score for the black team in the first half remains on that half of the pitch and plays for the white team in the second half.

Scoring

As normal; the last player can use hands to parry shots at the minigoal, and the goalkeeper changes teams at halftime.

Variations

1. Playing time and penalties can be increased or reduced.
2. The extra player can be moved to the other team, making the game eight versus eight.
3. An extra team, the green team, can replace the white team if there is no score after a set length of time. If the green team does not score either, they change again.

Coaching Points

During the second half, the black team should defend what it gained in the first half. This game focuses on how a team can consistently maintain a lead, so the emphasis is on the defensive tasks of the black team. Extra playing time is the penalty for errors that lead to goals, and it is therefore important for the individual players and the team to keep concentration and quality of work high. This applies, for example, to communication regarding cover, pressure on the player with the ball, and recovery play in the defensive zone.

The inequality of numbers (eight versus seven) in one half means the team that is superior in numbers should try to exploit this advantage by scoring, giving both teams some goals to work toward.

In variation one, the session can be made more time consuming (e.g., the second half can last 30 minutes or longer).

Variation two increases the probability of a draw at halftime, thereby putting more pressure on the black team in the second half.

In variation three, the black team is under more pressure, as it has to meet a fresh team.

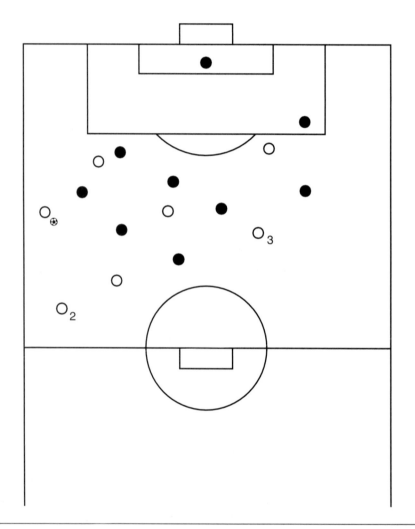

Figure 13.1   Bolt and lock.

CONCLUSION

In conclusion, we offer a few reflections on how we can truly gauge the effects of tactical training. Victories and defeats are not the only criteria we can measure a team's tactical quality against. In such an evaluation, it is important to base analysis on performances over a set period of time, perhaps one season. You can judge your long-term plan by taking a good look at the tactical goals the squad sets and observing how closely these are linked to training. At the same time, you should take into account the extent to which experience and changes due to tournament games have affected the present tactical climate. On an ongoing basis, you should maintain the general tactical aims while adjusting tactical issues in relation to day-to-day realities, such as squad changes, particular opponents, or the team's position in the tournament. You must employ this flexible thought process in order to keep on adjusting—and possibly reevaluating—the tactical plan. Your tactical role has succeeded when, in a winning team, the connection between your main tactical principles, the current game's tactical concept, and the team's performance is visible.

Tactical Opportunities

The introduction to the book *Soccer Systems & Strategies* describes Spain's defeat of the Danish in November 1993. This defeat prevented Denmark from qualifying for the 1994 World Cup in the United States. A great story to demonstrate the tactics of soccer is a description of, on one hand, Denmark's successful qualification for the 1998 World Cup Finals in France and, on the other hand, the team's successful participation in the World Cup. Most of the credit for this success goes to the management of the Danish team's tactics in the last two qualifiers against Croatia and Greece, as well as at the actual finals.

When Bo Johansson was appointed the Danish coach, he knew that the team's style and system of play was based on a 4-4-2 formation with the emphasis on playing in the opposition's half of the pitch. Denmark played like this through all the games until the penultimate qualifier—but introduced a surprising change in the system in the home game against Croatia. Bo Johansson abandoned the 4-4-2 system and the team adopted a 3-5-2 formation, with Michael Laudrup as a kind of hanging left wing. The formation, shown in figure 1, was to match the Croatian five-man midfield while allowing for Michael Laudrup's creative offensive chances. The Danish team played according to this tactic and won a handsome 3-1 victory. The implications of the final, deciding qualifier between Greece and Denmark were clear to both teams: If Denmark won or drew, the team would be through to the World Cup Finals in France during the summer of 1998, while only a Greek victory would be enough for first place in the group and automatic qualification.

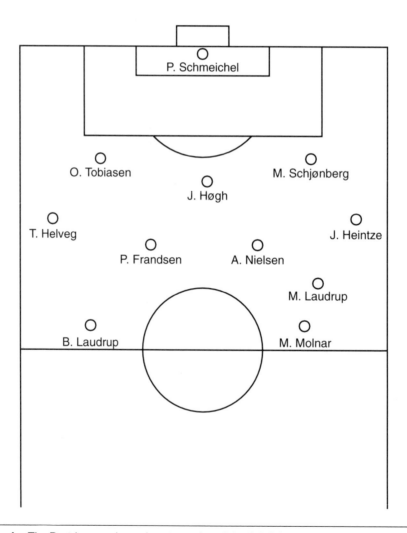

Figure 1 The Danish team changed tactics and used this 3-5-2 formation against Croatia.

The Danish style of play during the mid-1980s was popularly called "dynamite soccer." This referred to the team's sparkling, creative style of play which gave rise to several unforgettable performances at the 1986 World Cup. These have now been supplanted in people's memories by Denmark's last two games at the 1998 World Cup, against Nigeria and Brazil respectively.

In his tactical thinking, Bo Johansson was adamant that the Danish defensive game must not have holes near the back. The Greeks would have to attack strongly, and this could best be balanced against complete cover widthwise in the Danish defense. At the same time, this attack also opened up the chances of Danish counterattacks, the old Danish trademark. The match finished 0-0, confirming Denmark's place at the 1998 World Cup Finals in France—and providing several examples of the tactical aspect of the coach's role in a constant analytical and management process.

Denmark's World Cup Tactics

The Danish performance at the 1998 World Cup can be divided into two parts. The introductory qualifying games were fairly mediocre, but the second round and the quarterfinal were extremely impressive. How could a team change so drastically? It is possible to explain this by analyzing the tactical context.

The Danish team's performances in the games leading up to the World Cup caused doubt about the team's viability. Particularly worrisome was the fact that the hitherto-successful defense had become so disjointed that it seemed to pose no problems for opponents. The limited number of goals the Danish attackers were scoring did not help alleviate this lack of optimism.

Since the initial games in the World Cup Finals are arranged as group games, it is vital for a team to keep a clean sheet as far as possible. In this defensive crisis, it was therefore understandable from a tactical point of view that Denmark's first two group games were based on a defensive 4-4-2 formation, even if the opponents, Saudi Arabia and South Africa, were not exactly terrifying. With four points after the first two games and a rehabilitated central defense, the way was now clear for a more pronounced offensive. This meant that in the game against France, Michael Laudrup in particular had to get forward quickly, ahead of the other three midfielders, to create more depth in attack. This succeeded only to a certain extent, but with an honorable defeat the Danes had secured their place in the second round, while their starting formation against Nigeria was clear. It meant, however, that they had to change their basic strategy: instead of concentrating on their own weaknesses, they were now gambling on exploiting those of the opposition.

Nigeria's Achilles' heel was its defense, including the goalkeeper, and Bo Johansson astutely changed his strategy, arranging the Danish starting lineup in a 4-3-3 formation. In reality, however, the team was organized in a 4-3-1-2 formation (see figure 2 on page 214). Michael Laudrup was positioned 10 to 15 meters ahead of the other three midfielders, and his defensive role was very different from that in a 4-4-2 formation.

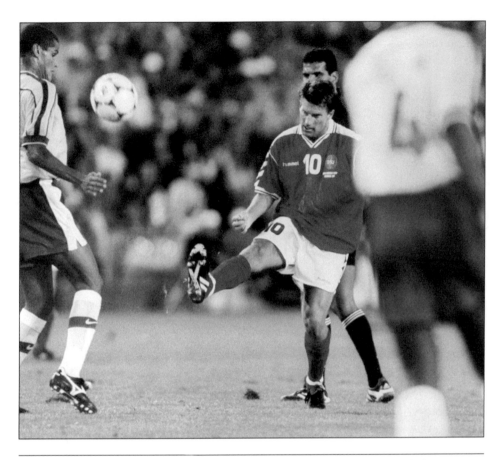

The fascinating thing about soccer is its unpredictability as the game unfolds randomly before our eyes. There are perfect moments in team tactics and individual actions. Take, for example, the 1998 World Cup and Michael Laudrup setting up Ebbe Sand's goal against Nigeria, after which the team's performance continued—with no goals, unfortunately—in the unforgettable quarterfinal game against Brazil.

This was the context behind a great performance by the Danish team, followed by an even better one against Brazil. The Danish World Cup team's transformation from "donkey" to "dynamite" was due to vital tactical maneuvers on the part of the coach.

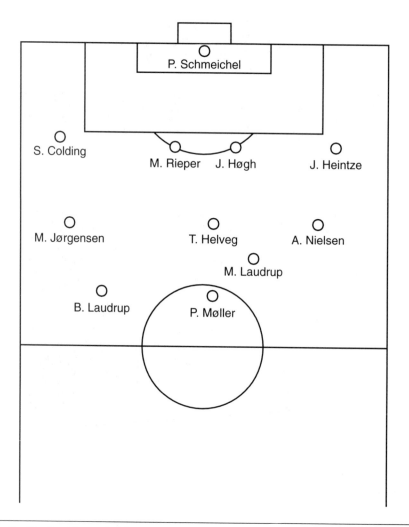

Figure 2 The Danish team's 4-3-1-2 formation against Nigeria.

ABOUT
THE AUTHORS

Jens Bangsbo has been playing and coaching soccer for more than 35 years. He spent 15 years as a top-level player in Denmark, playing more than 400 matches in the top Danish league. In international play, he represented Denmark as both a youth player and as a member of the "A" national team.

Bangsbo has been an instructor at the Danish Football Association since 1986 and is an assistant head coach for the Juventus soccer club in Italy. He has published more than 100 articles on soccer and conditioning, and he has written several books, including *Soccer Systems & Strategies.*

Birger Peitersen is also one of Denmark's top soccer figures, having coached the Danish Women's national team and the national champions of the men's league, and also serving as staff coach of the Danish Football Federation. In 1982, he received the highest coaching award in Denmark, the Diploma in Elite Soccer Coaching.

Peitersen was the expert commentator for International European Matches on Danish television in the UEFA Champions League and for Danish radio at the World Cup in 1990 and 1998 and the European Championships in 1992 and 1996.

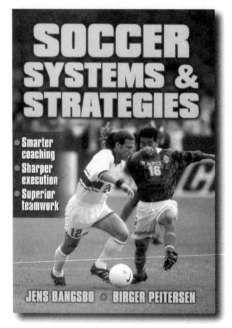